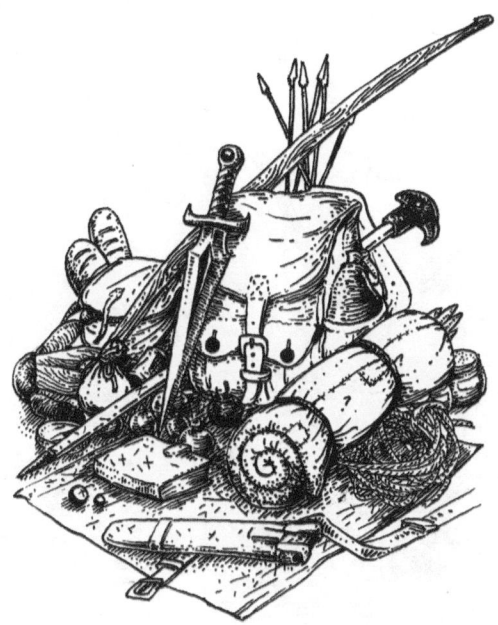

Adventure begins

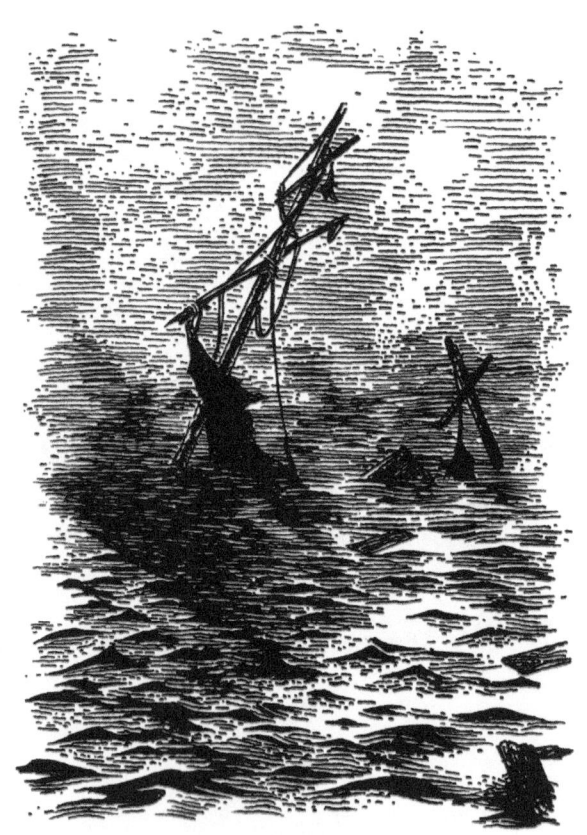

Lost at sea

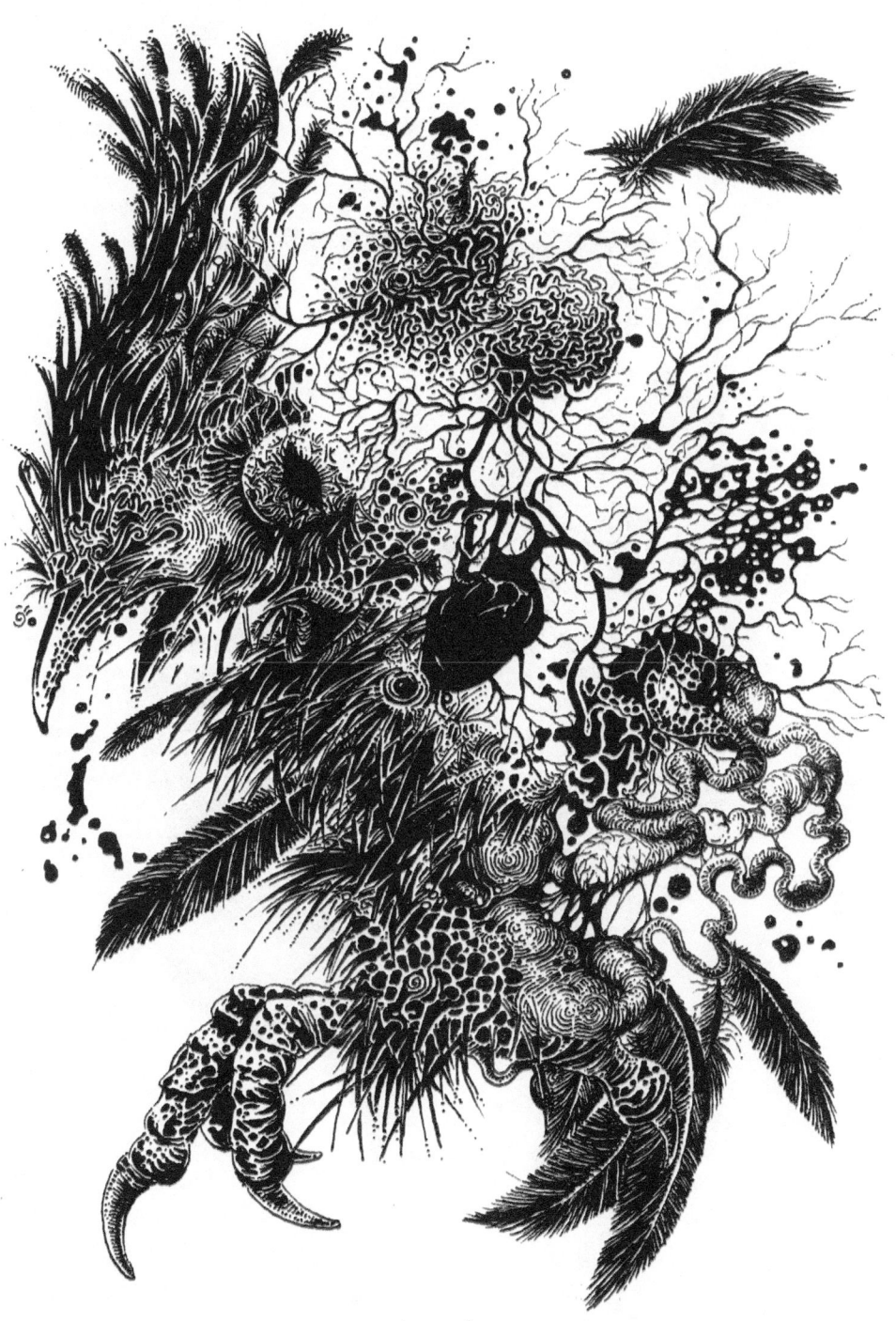

Innards

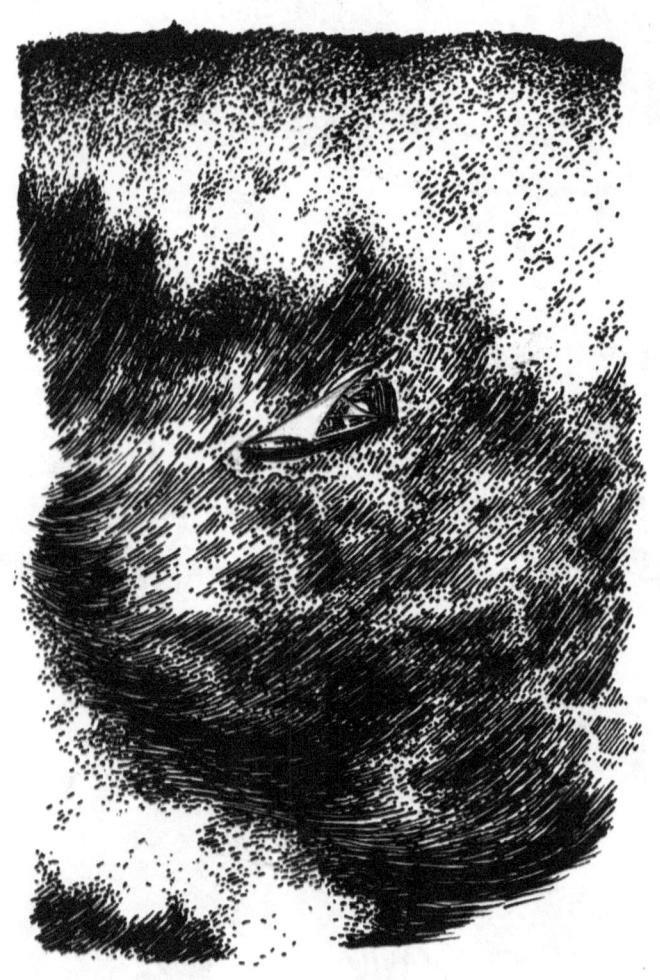

Lost at sea 2

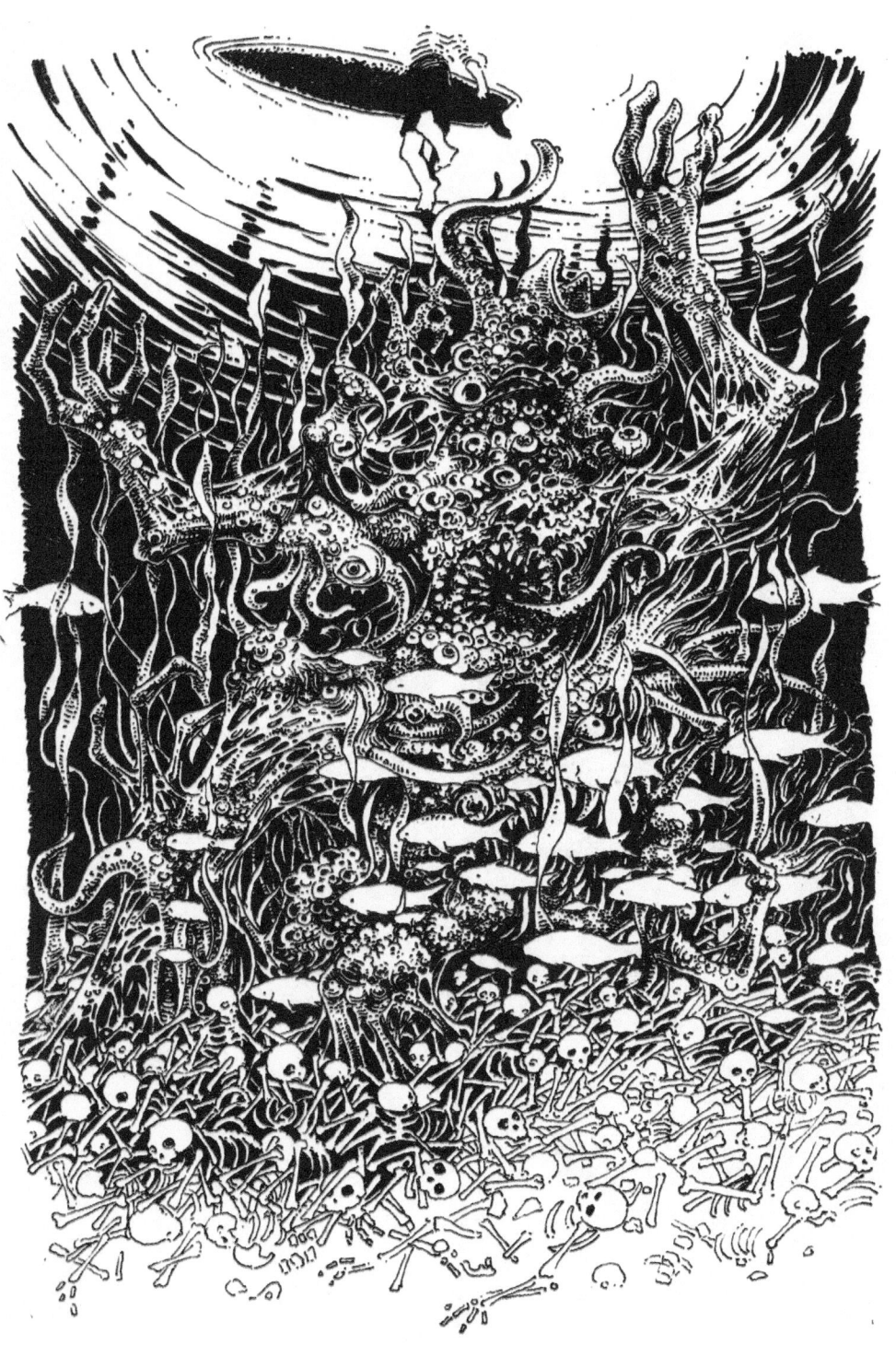

Beneath the surface

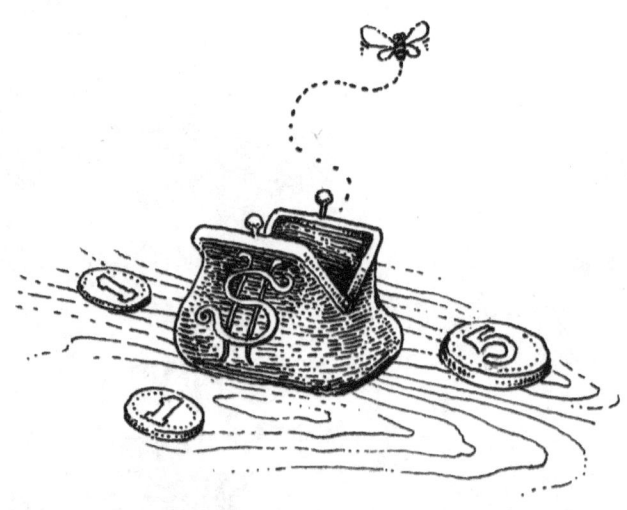

The little blue fairy woke up one day
and thought "Time to get a job".

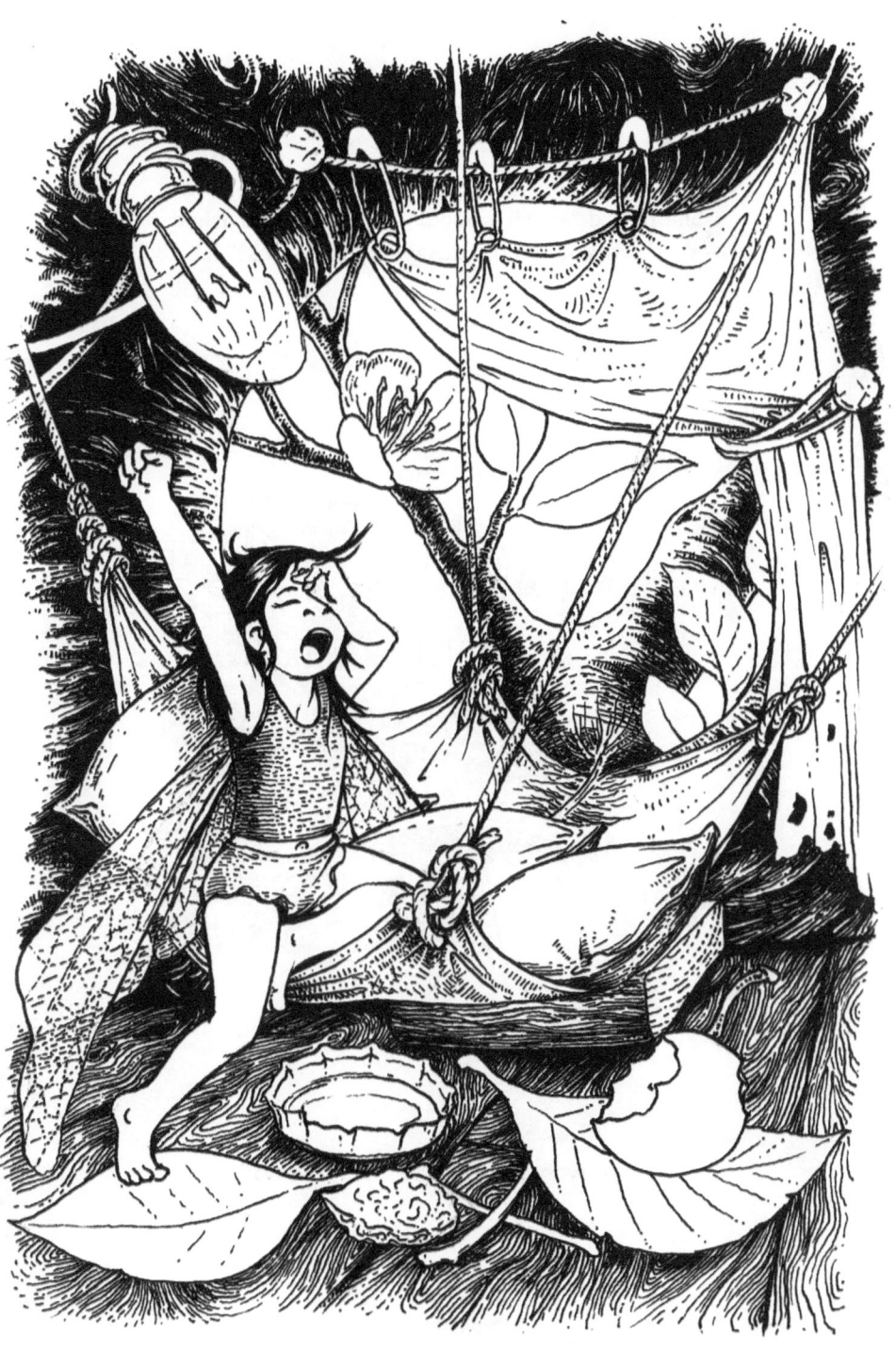

She flew down to a building company and asked
"Do you need a designer for houses?".

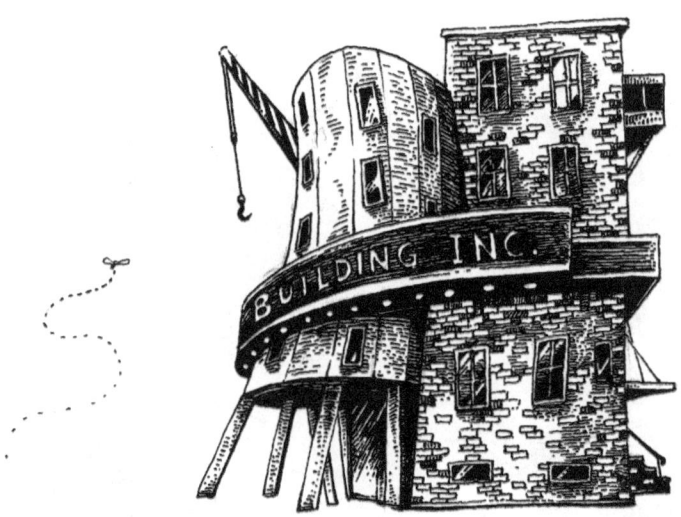

The woman in charge said "We do."

She directed the little blue fairy to a
small room of animal workers and said
"These will be your workers".

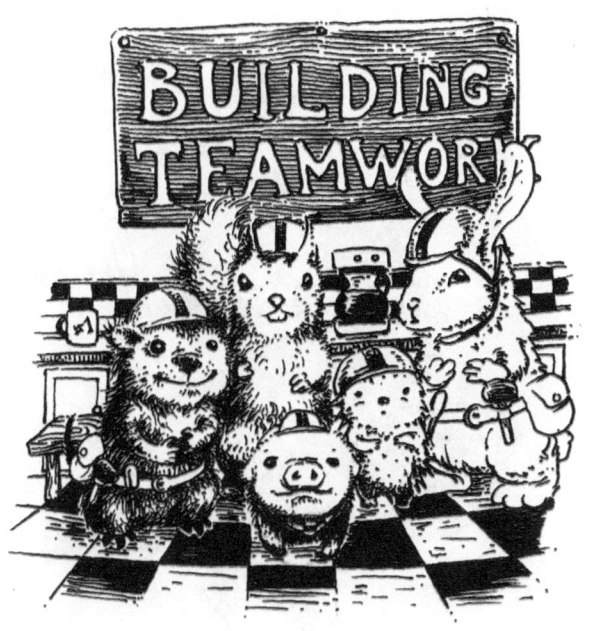

The fairy's first client was a bird.

He wanted a house with five bedrooms,
three bathrooms, and a hot tub room.
He also wanted his house to be on an apple tree.

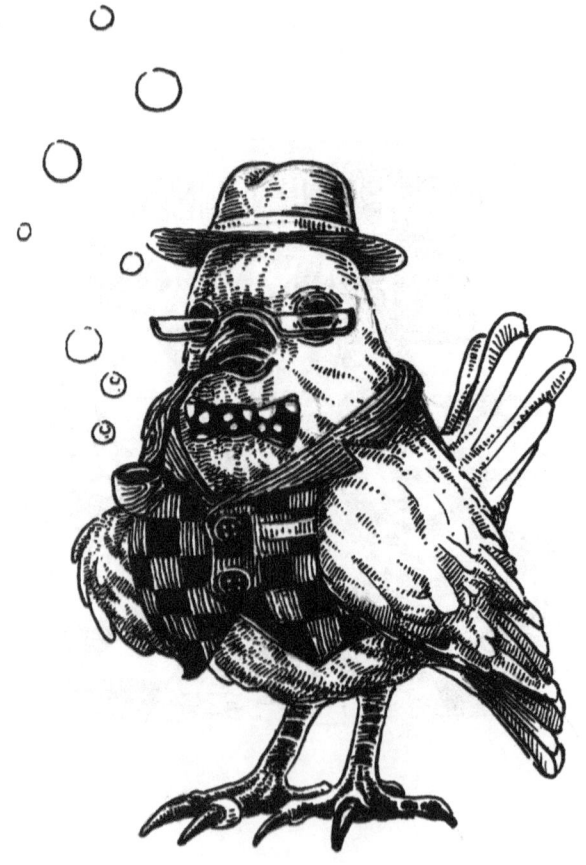

Little blue fairy searched all the nearby apple orchards for days, but she couldn't find an apple tree without squirrels or birds already living in it.

apple tree|

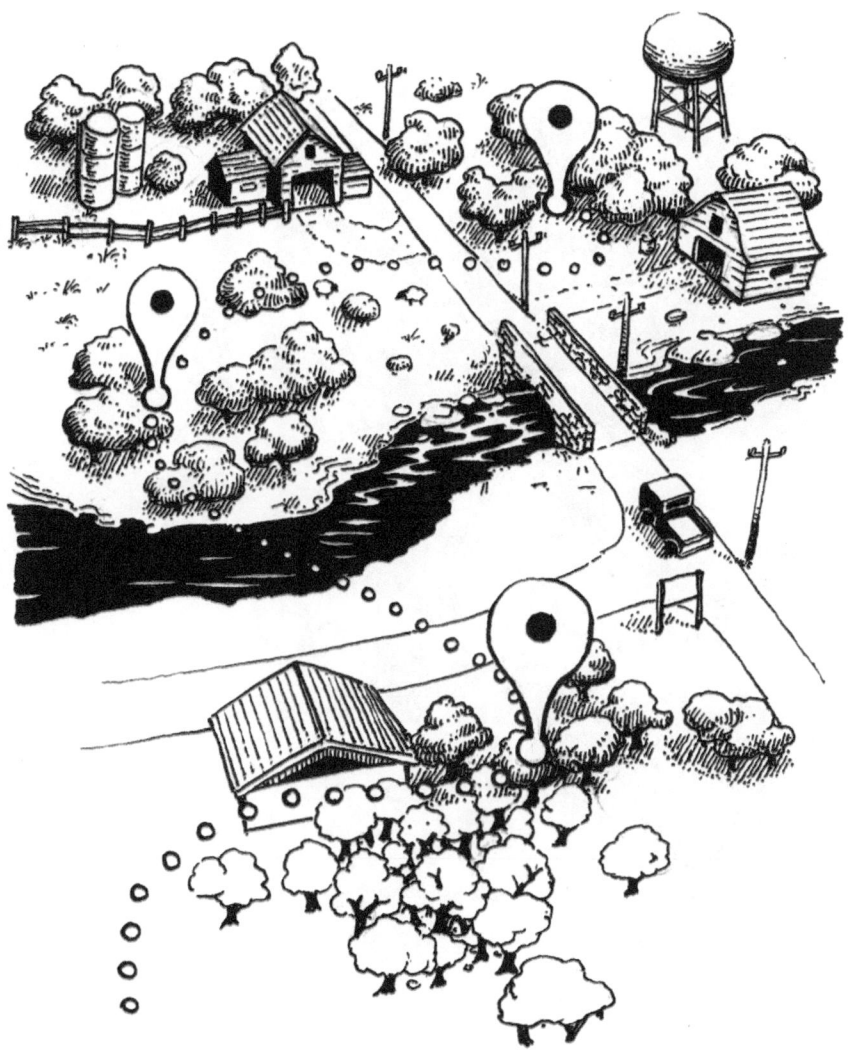

Then she saw a perfect nine years old apple tree on a hill
in a nearby park. Mr.Bird came to exam the tree,
and said it's perfect.

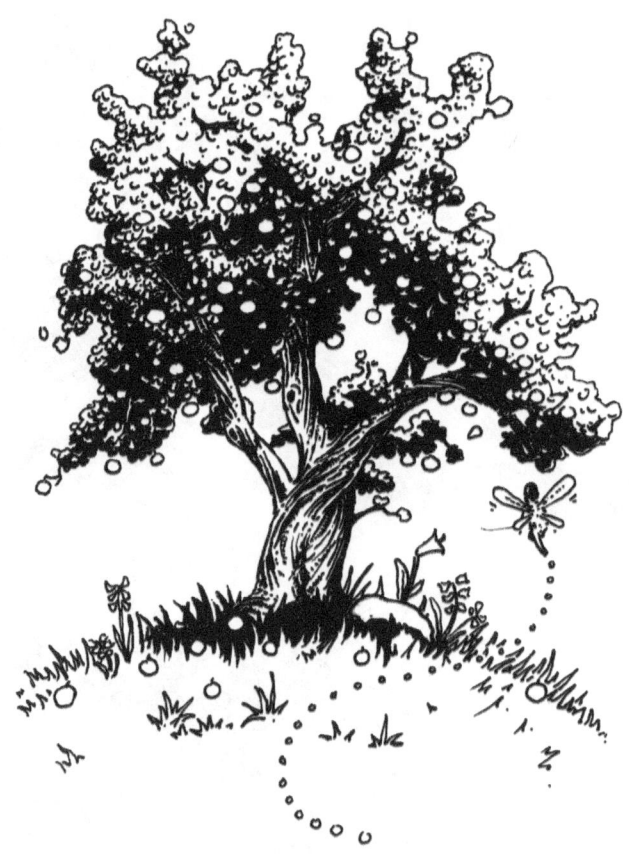

Mr. Bird also gave her some photos of the type of houses he likes. "I want my house exact like these." It was very complicated because the houses in his photos were all very fancy.

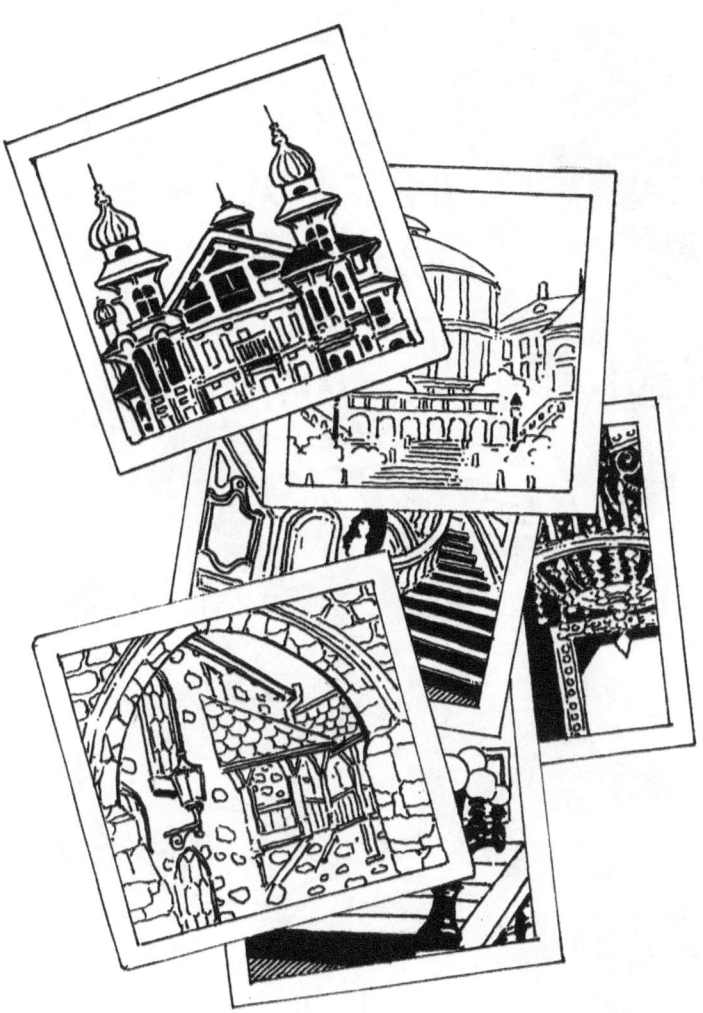

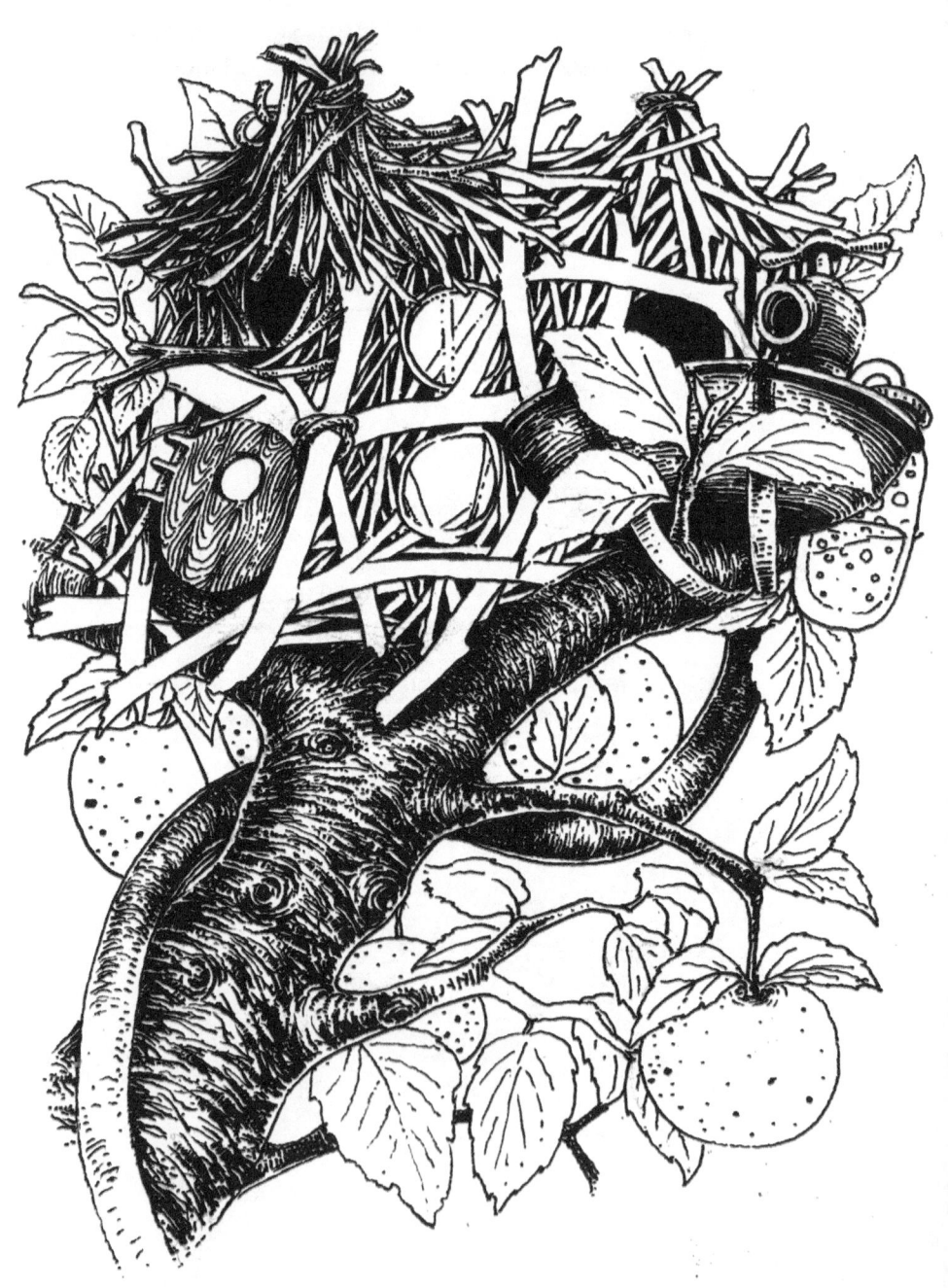

Little blue fairy told her boss she needed special workers and tools for fancy houses, but the company didn't have any.

She started building right away the very next morning. She had a meeting to tell them what to do and where to do it.

It worked out ok at first, but then a lot of the crew got the flu and she was left with only two people.

She decided she should just wait for her crew to get better, but they kept getting worse. After a while Mr. Bird was furious that the tree house was still just a bundle of sticks.

Little blue fairy told her boss all about the sick builders. The boss lady said she will try to get more workers, but little blue fairy was sure that there won't be builders good enough for the job.

One afternoon her boss showed up unexpectedly. She had come to tell little blue fairy some good news. She found more builders!

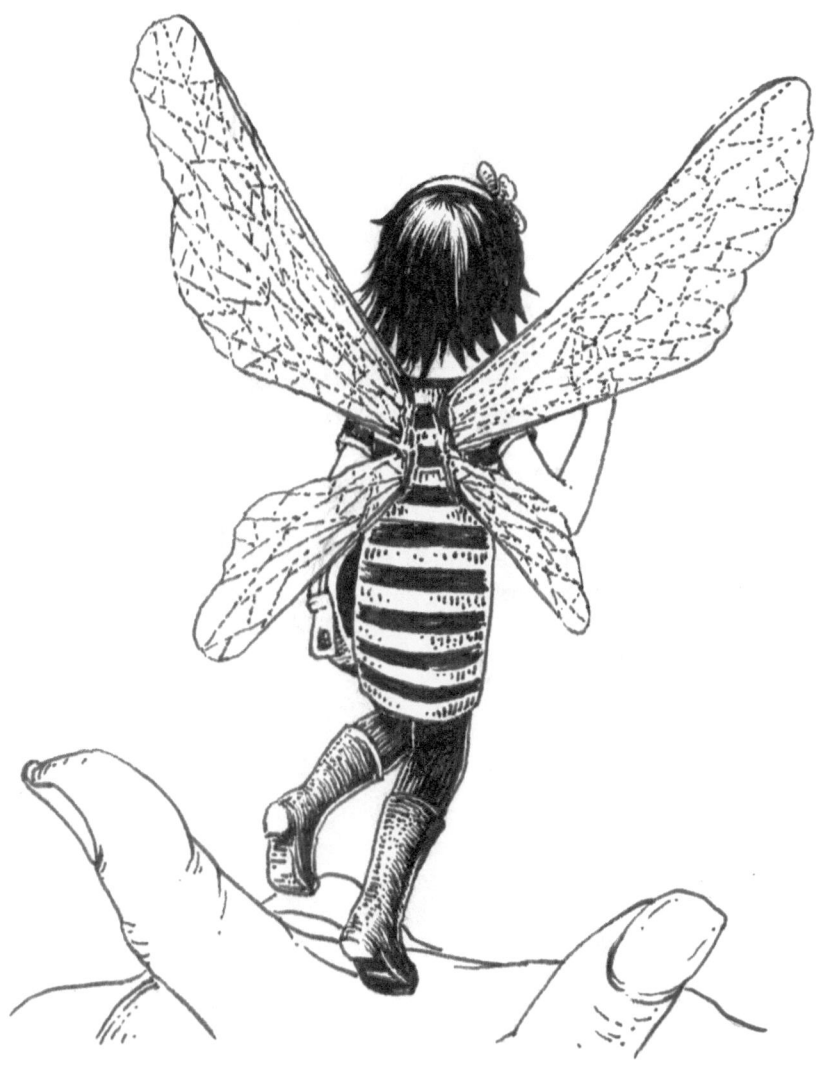

The next morning her new workers came to the tree. To her surprise Mr. Bird was in the group. It turns out Mr.Bird needed to make more money to buy the hot tub. He was astonished that he was building his own house.

After making a lot of mistakes, Mr. Bird finally saw how hard it was to build a huge fancy house on an apple tree. He apologised and agreed to make the house simpler.

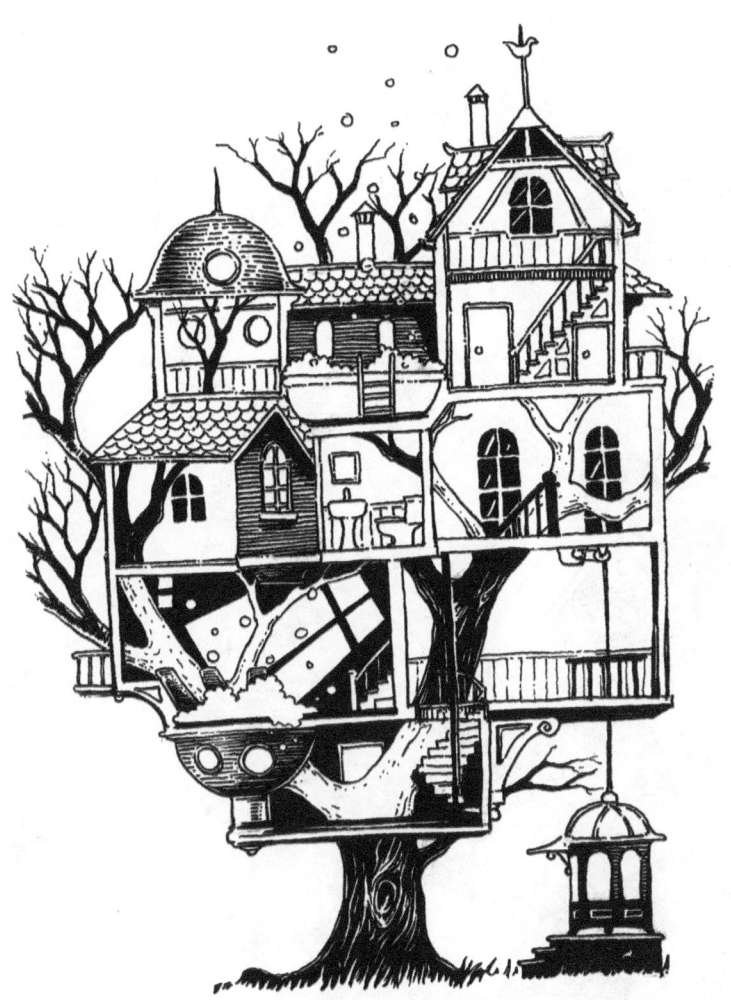

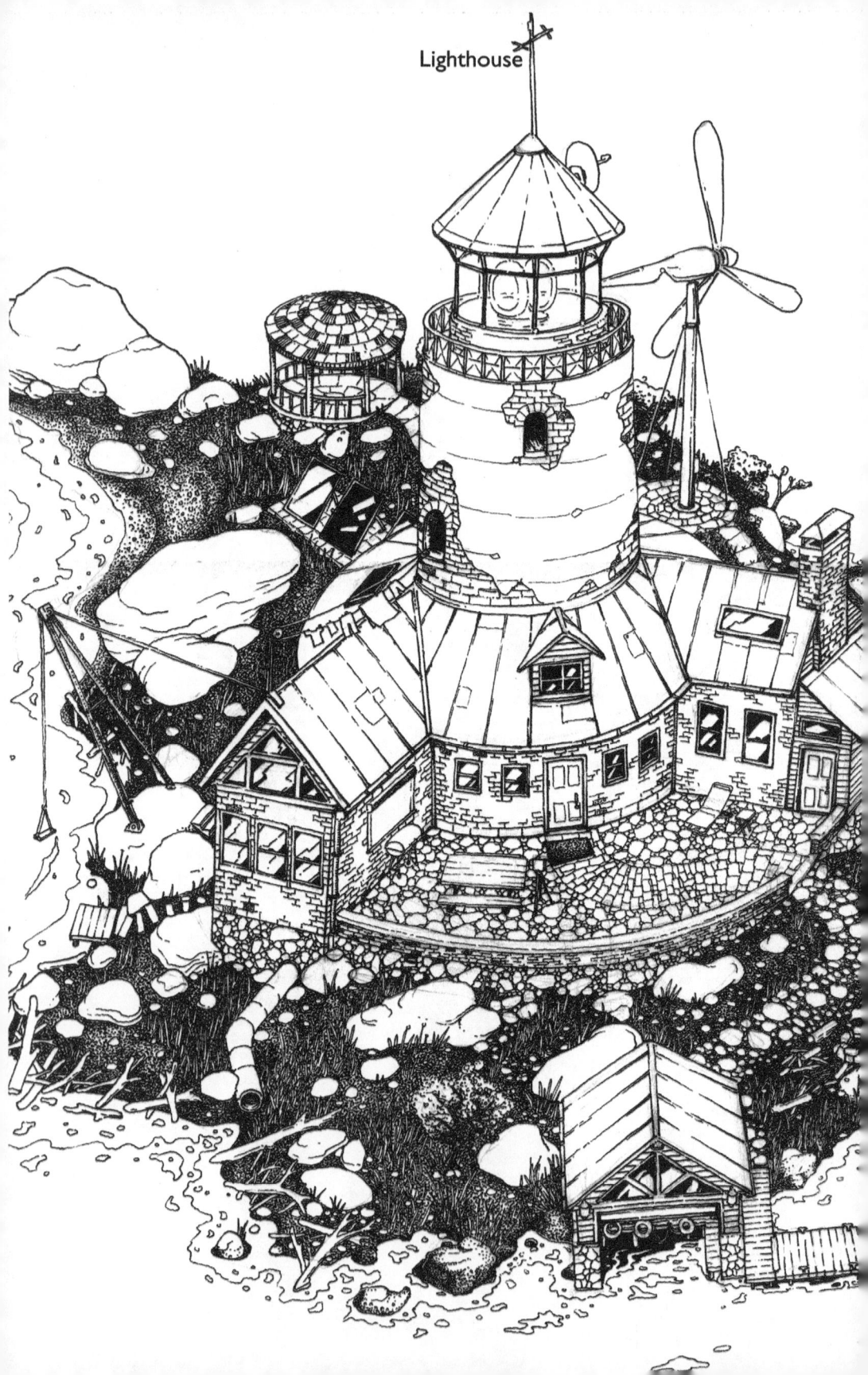

Lighthouse

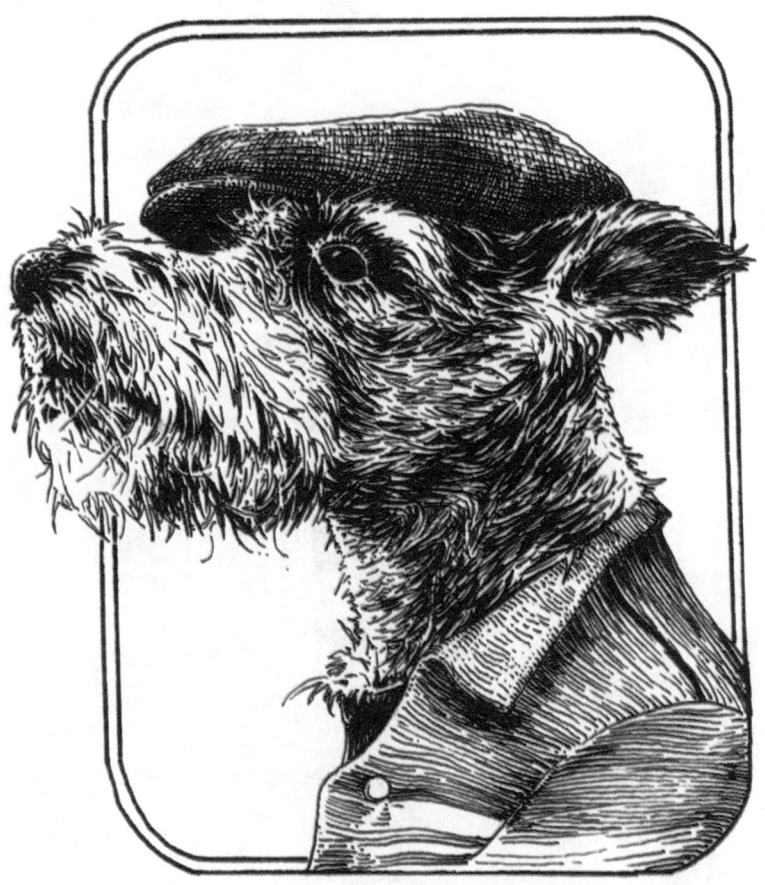

Terrier

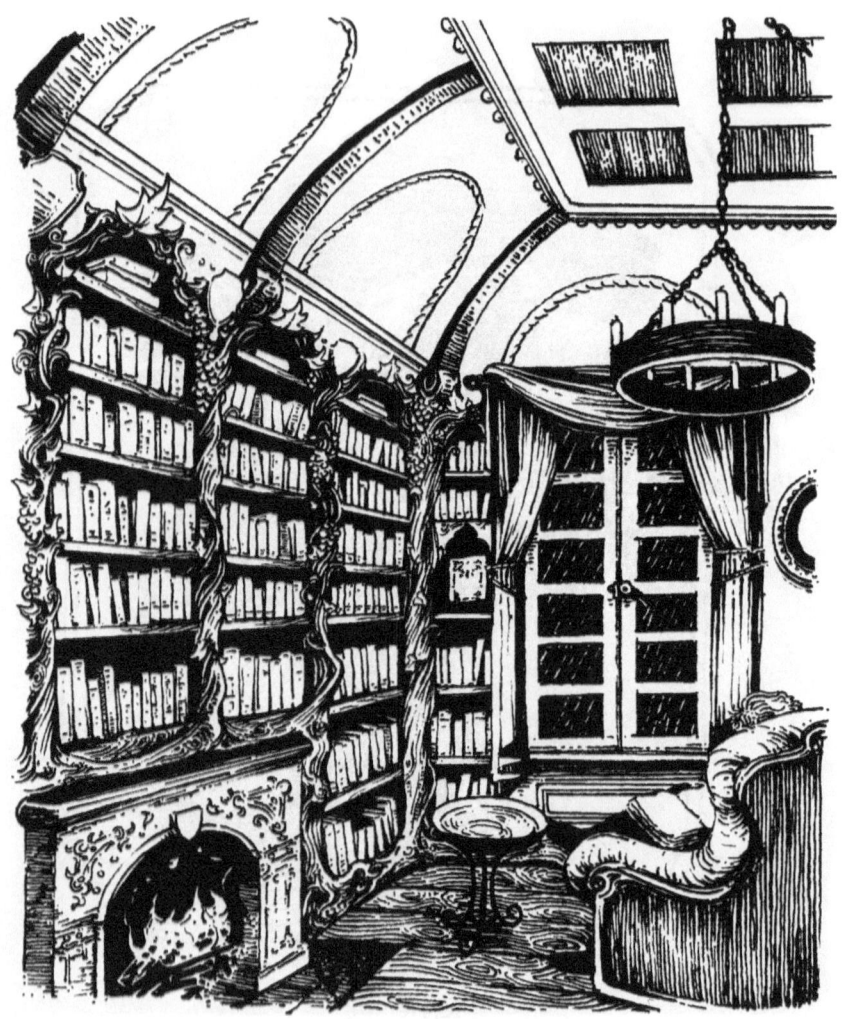

Mr. Norrell's library

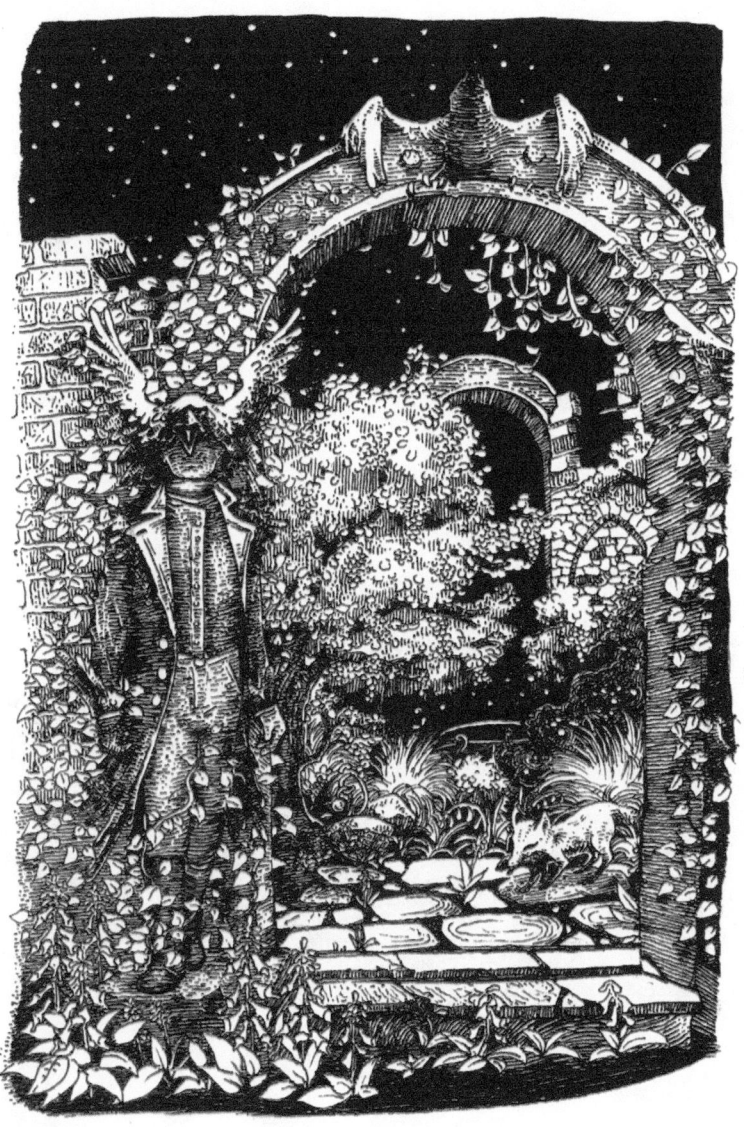

Raven King doorway

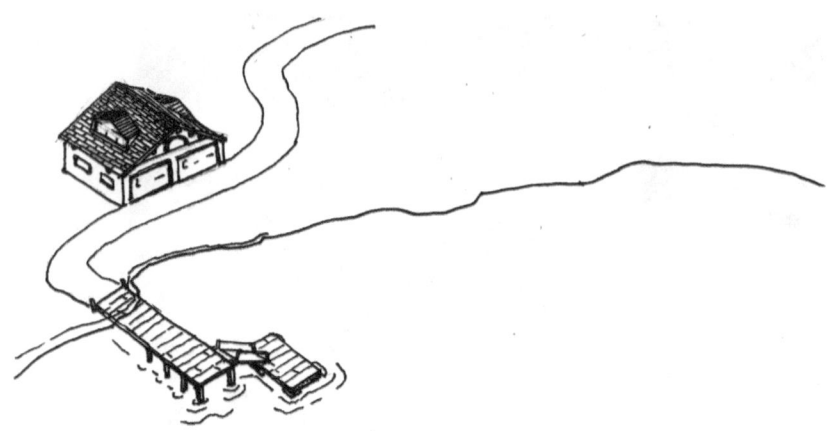

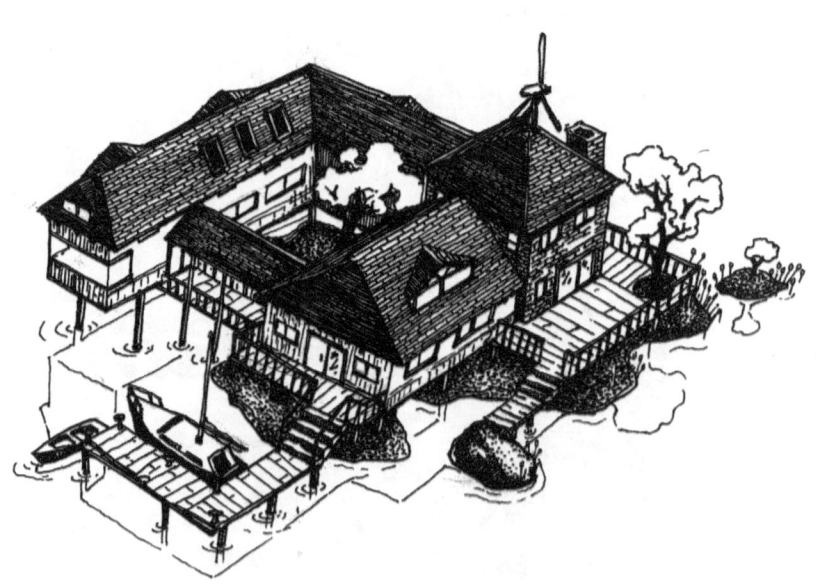

House on the lake

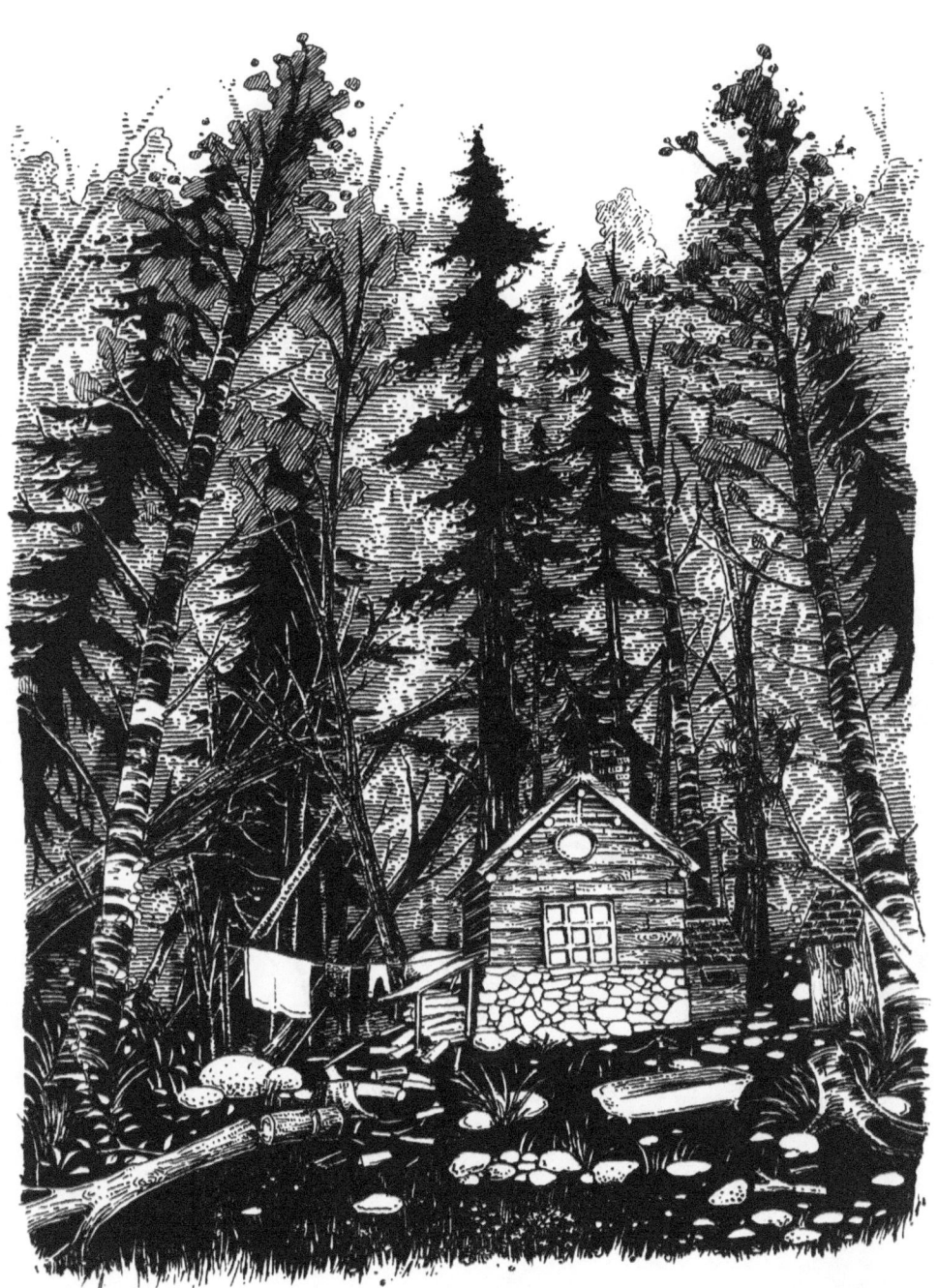

House in the woods

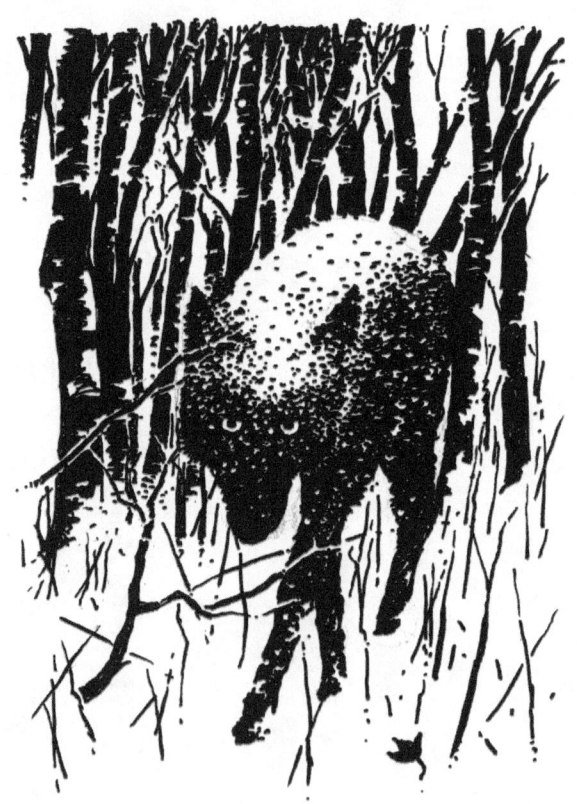

Wolf in snowfall

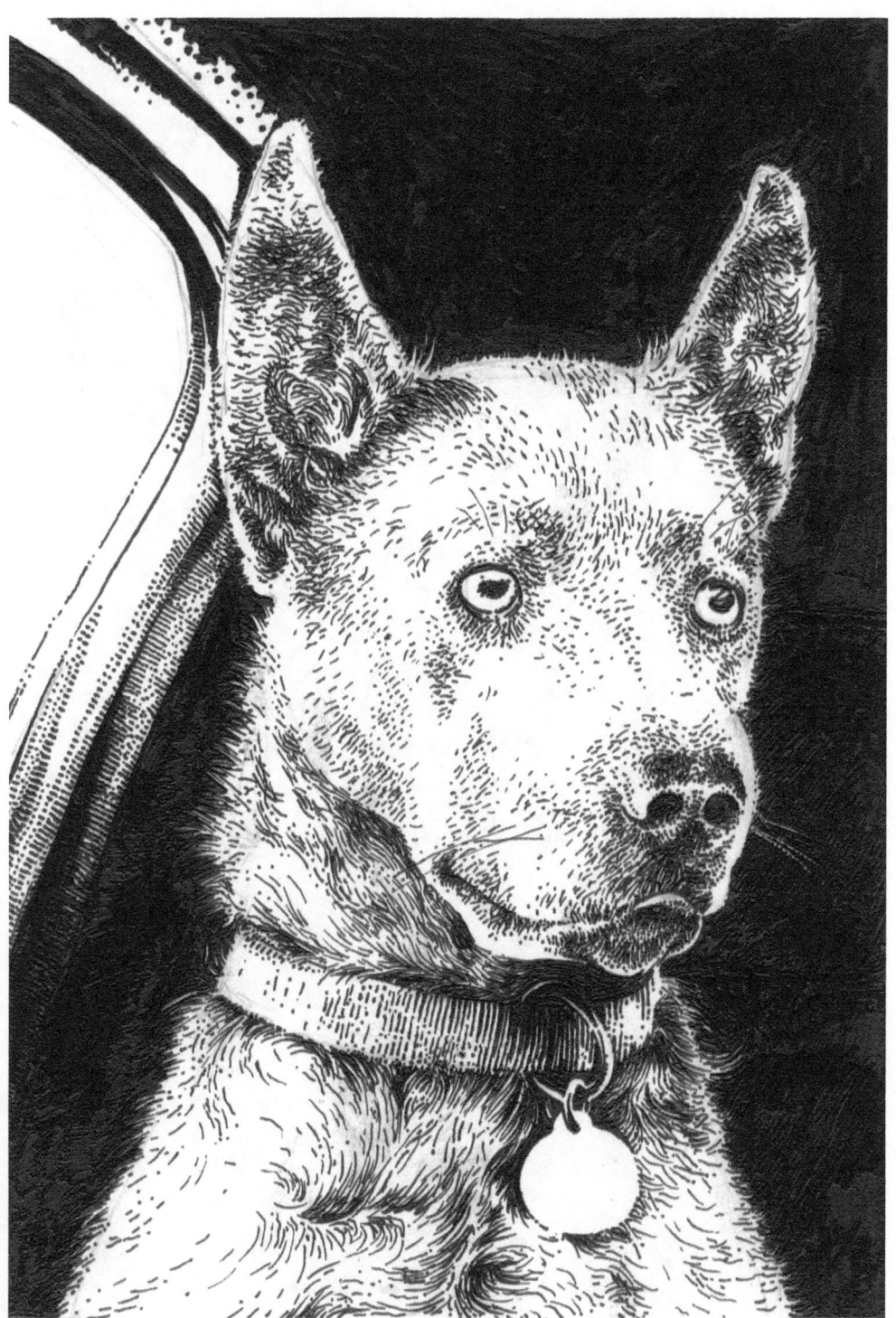

Dog

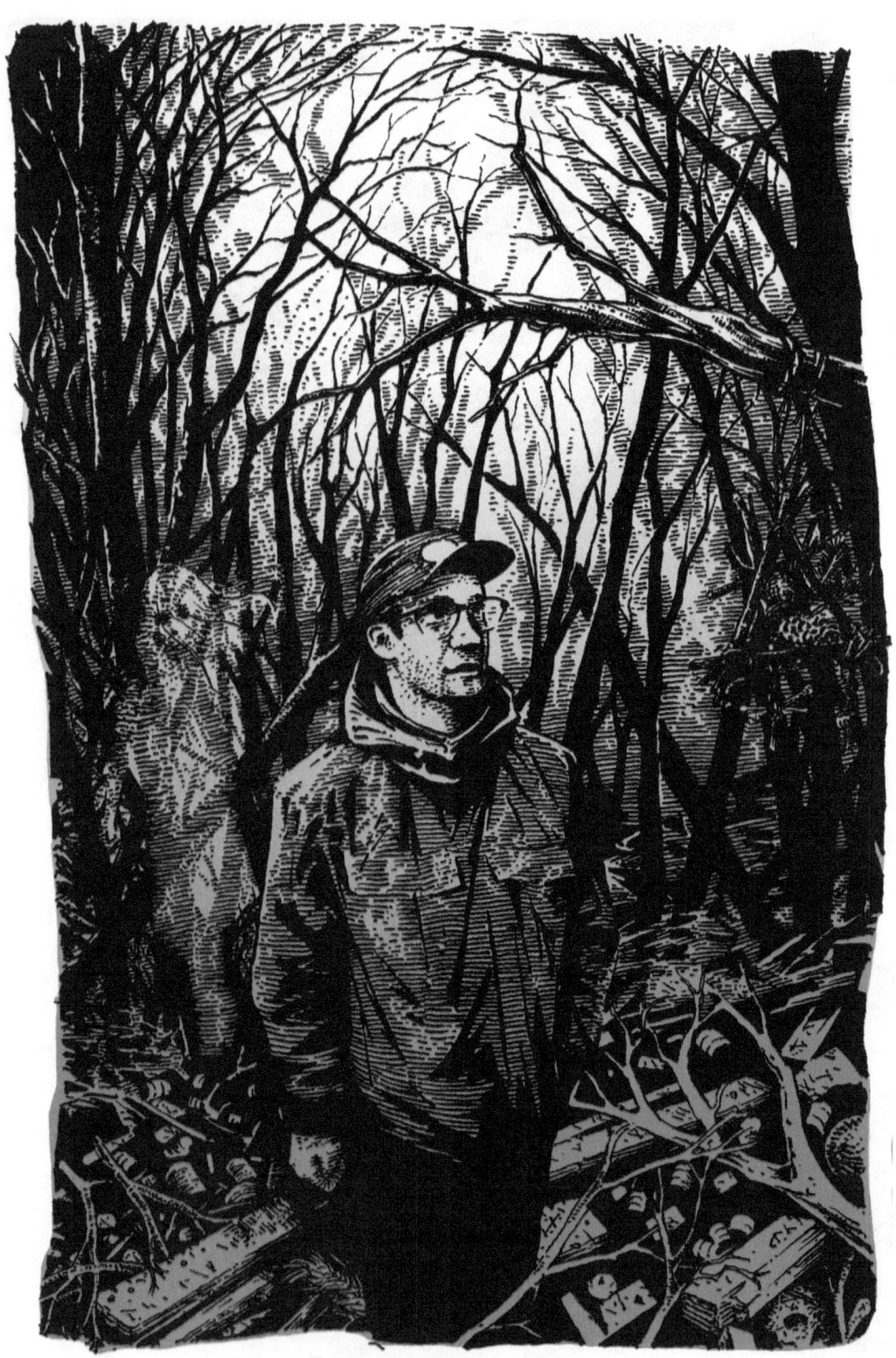

Encounter in the woods

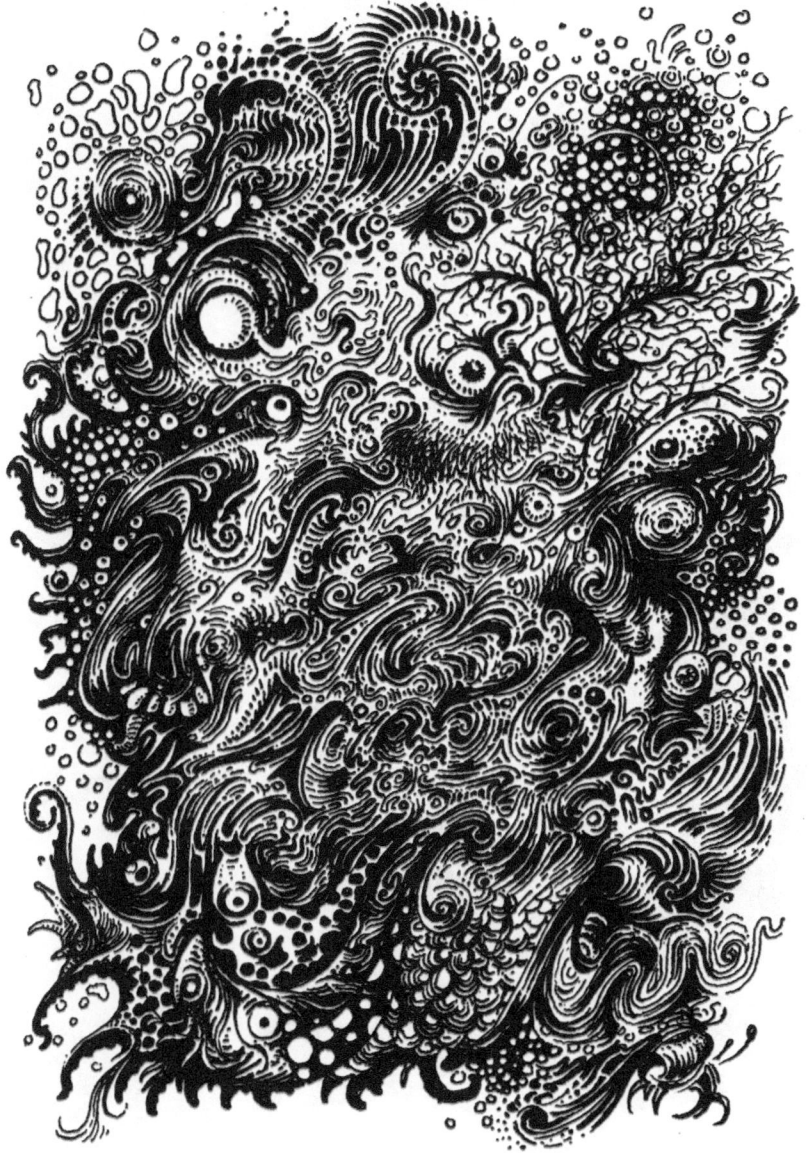

Anxiety

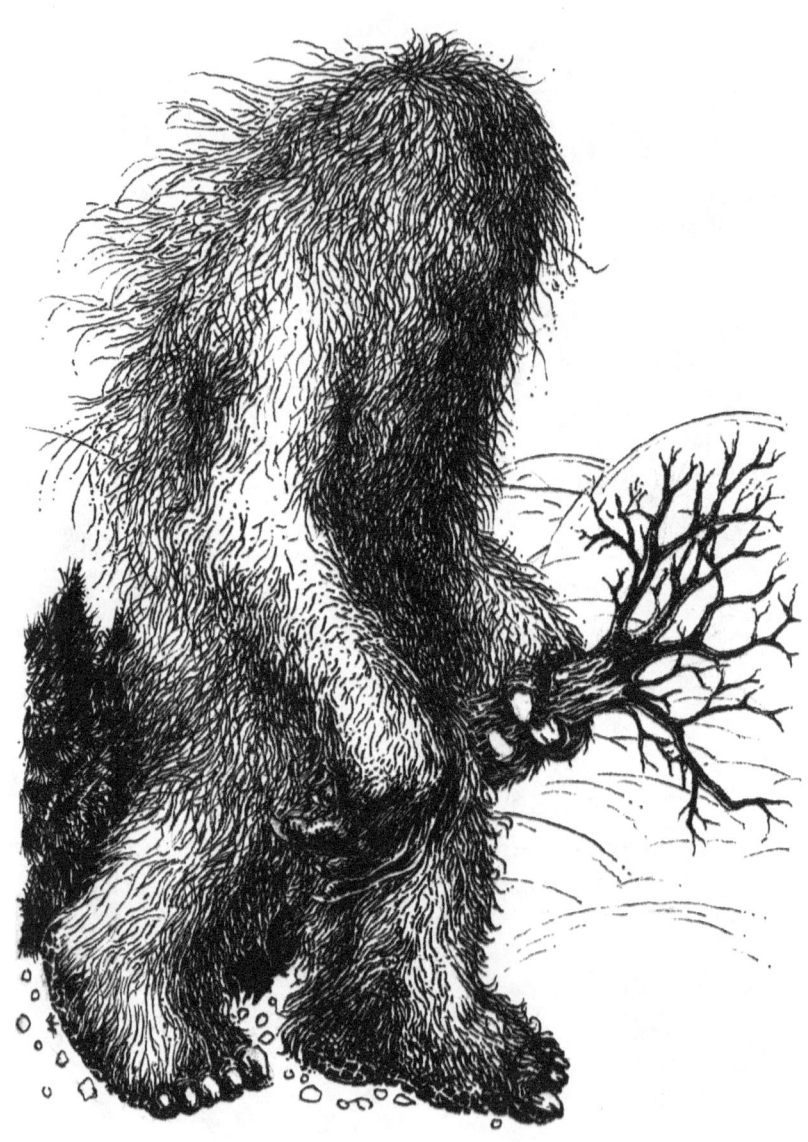

Snowman

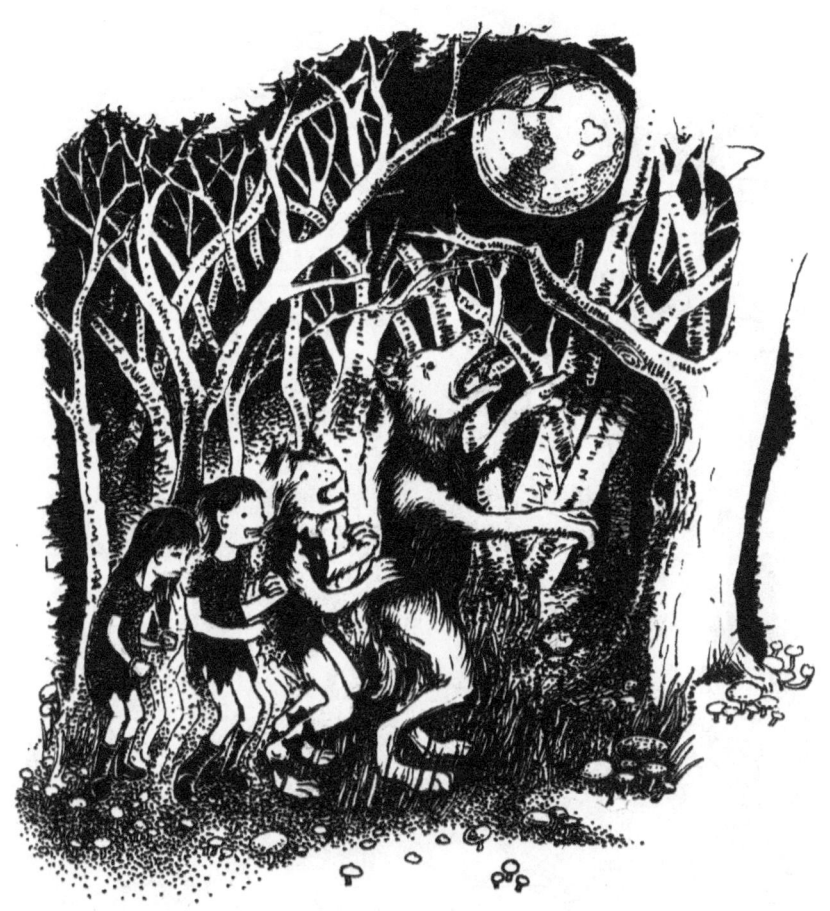

Wolf girl

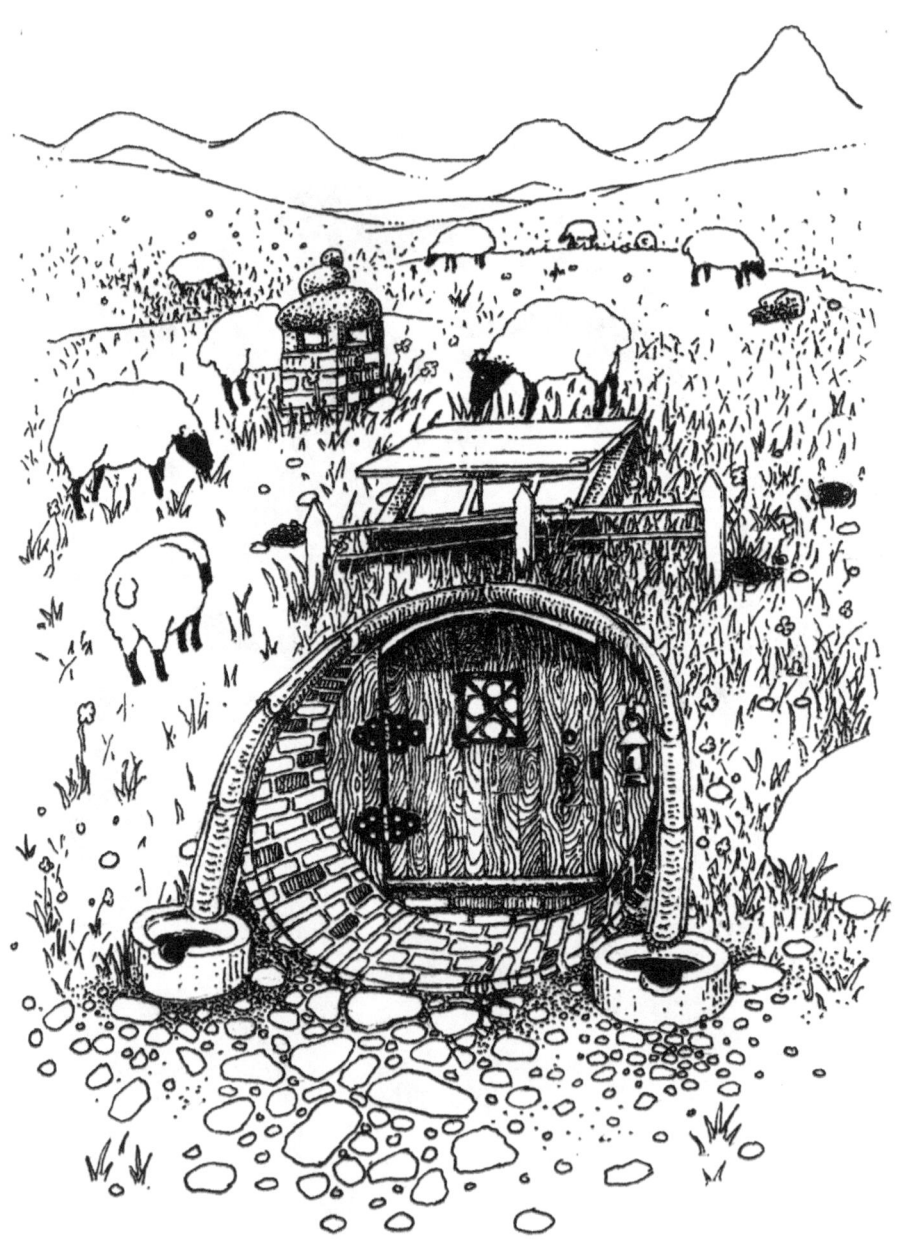

Shepard's hole - outside

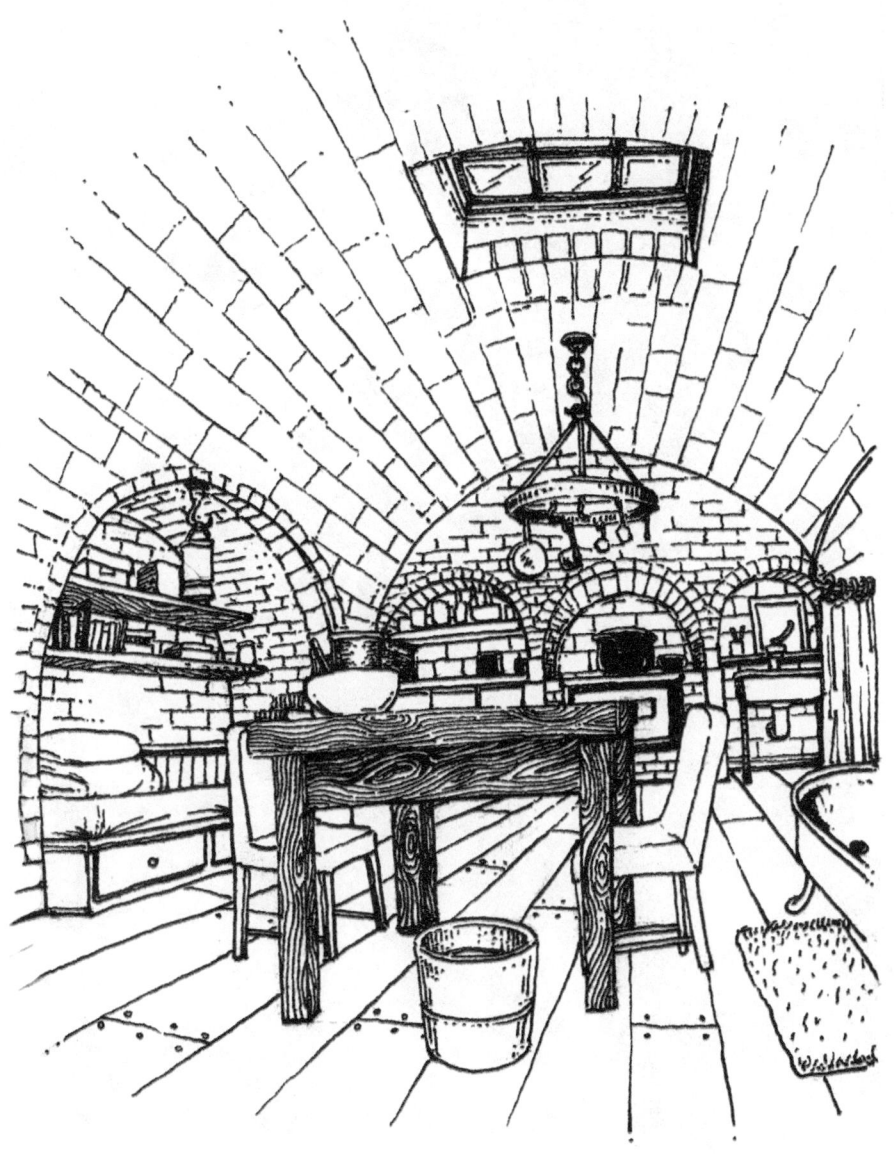

Shepard's hole - inside

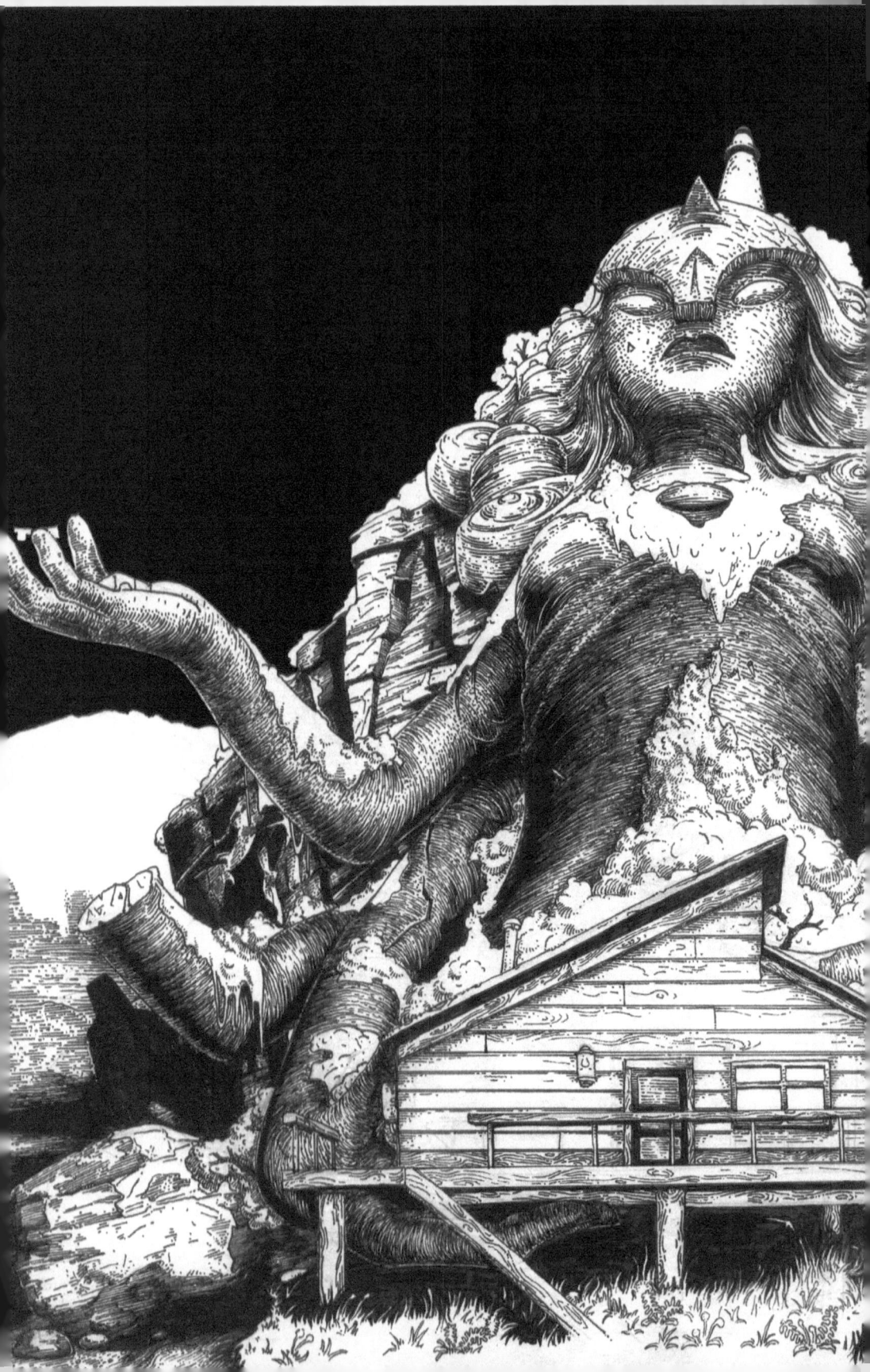

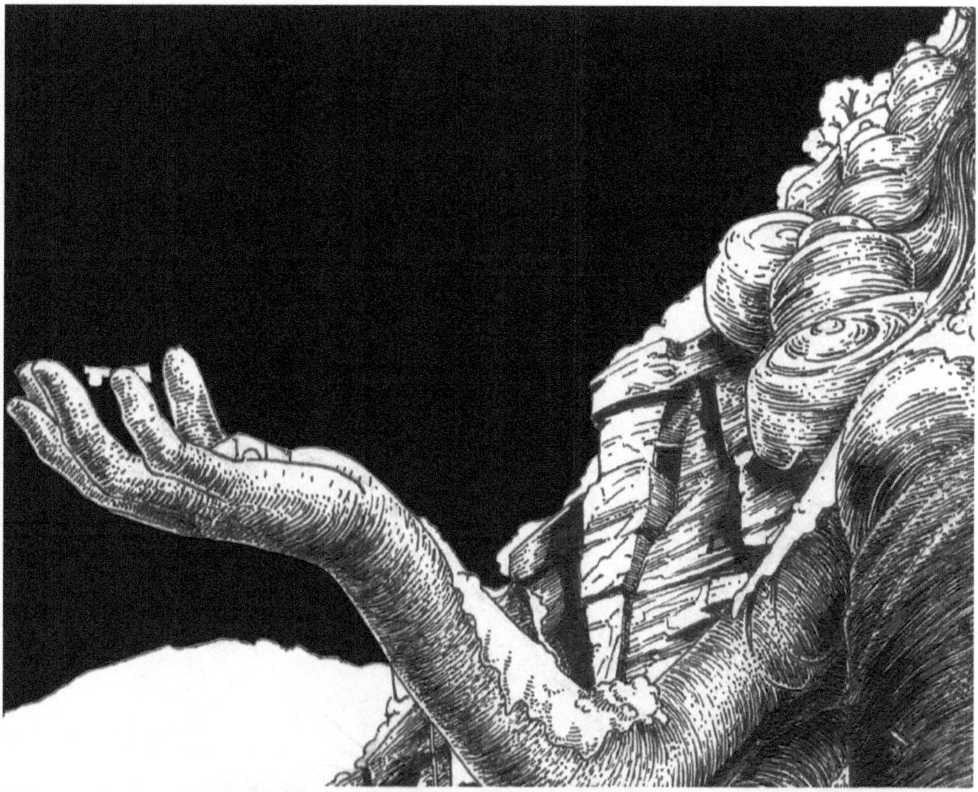

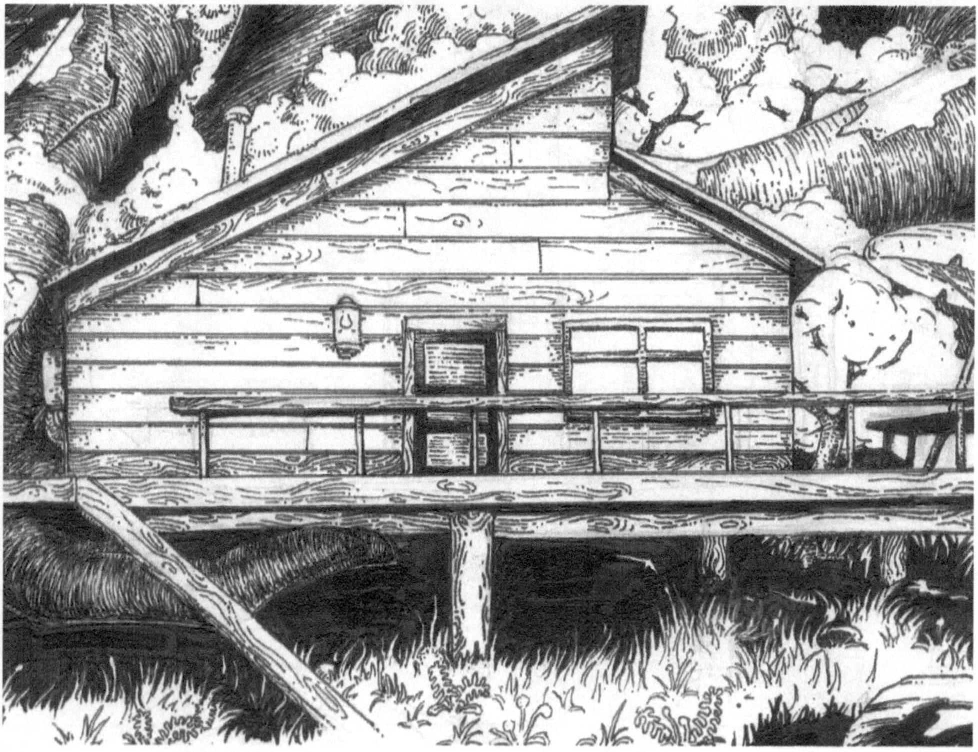

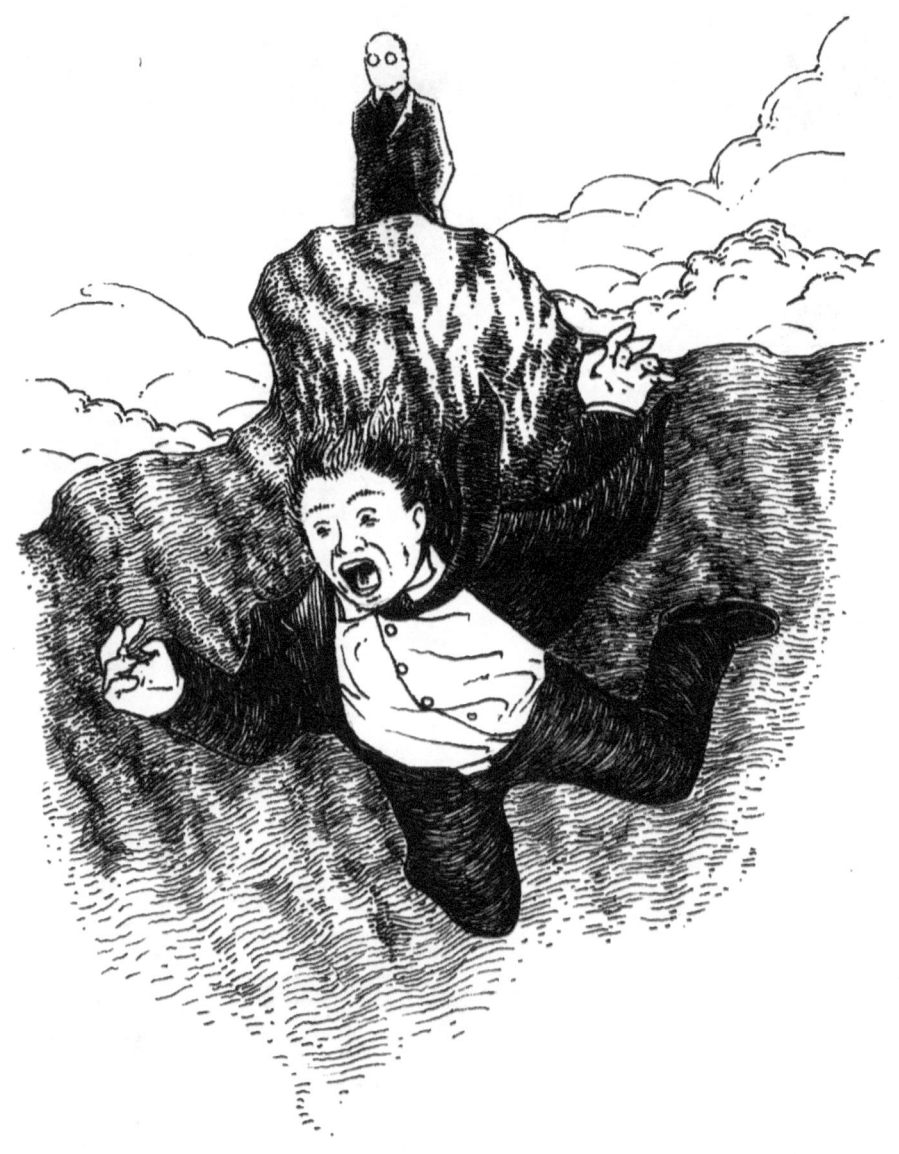

Over the cliff

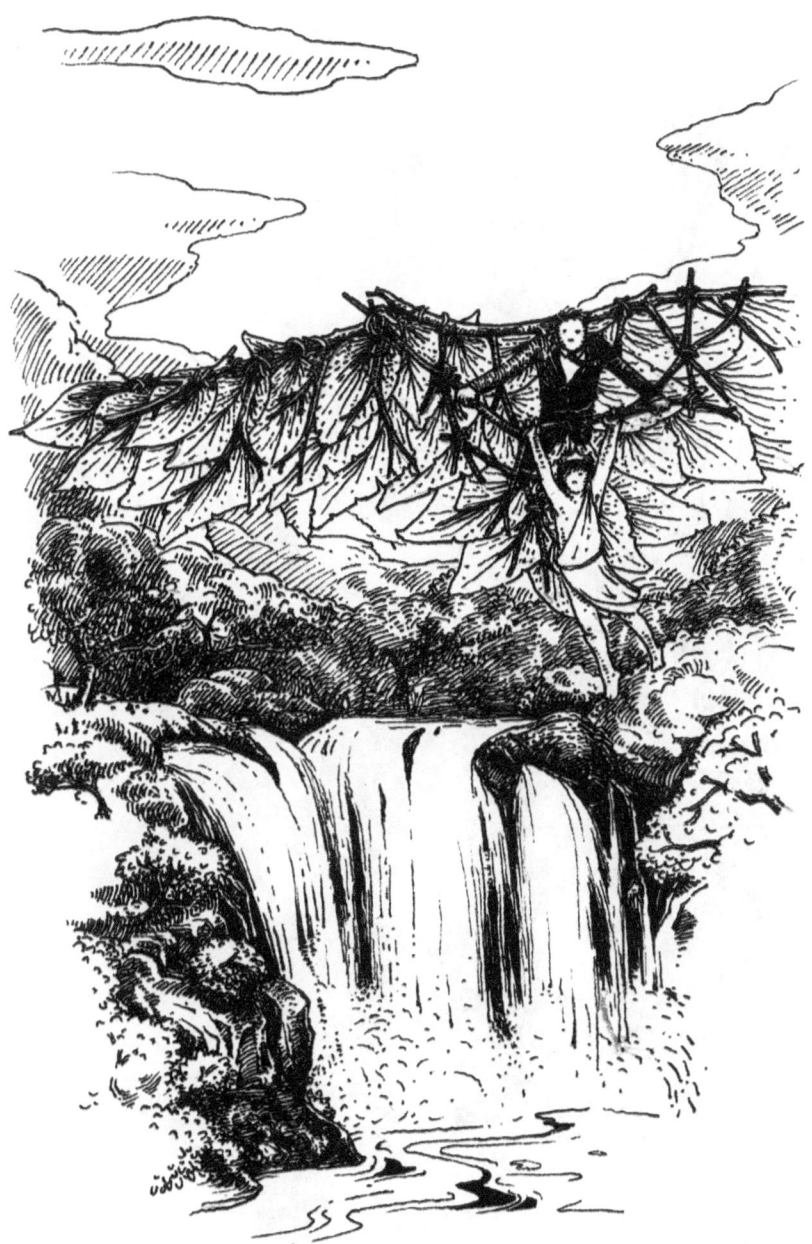

Fly through the waterfall

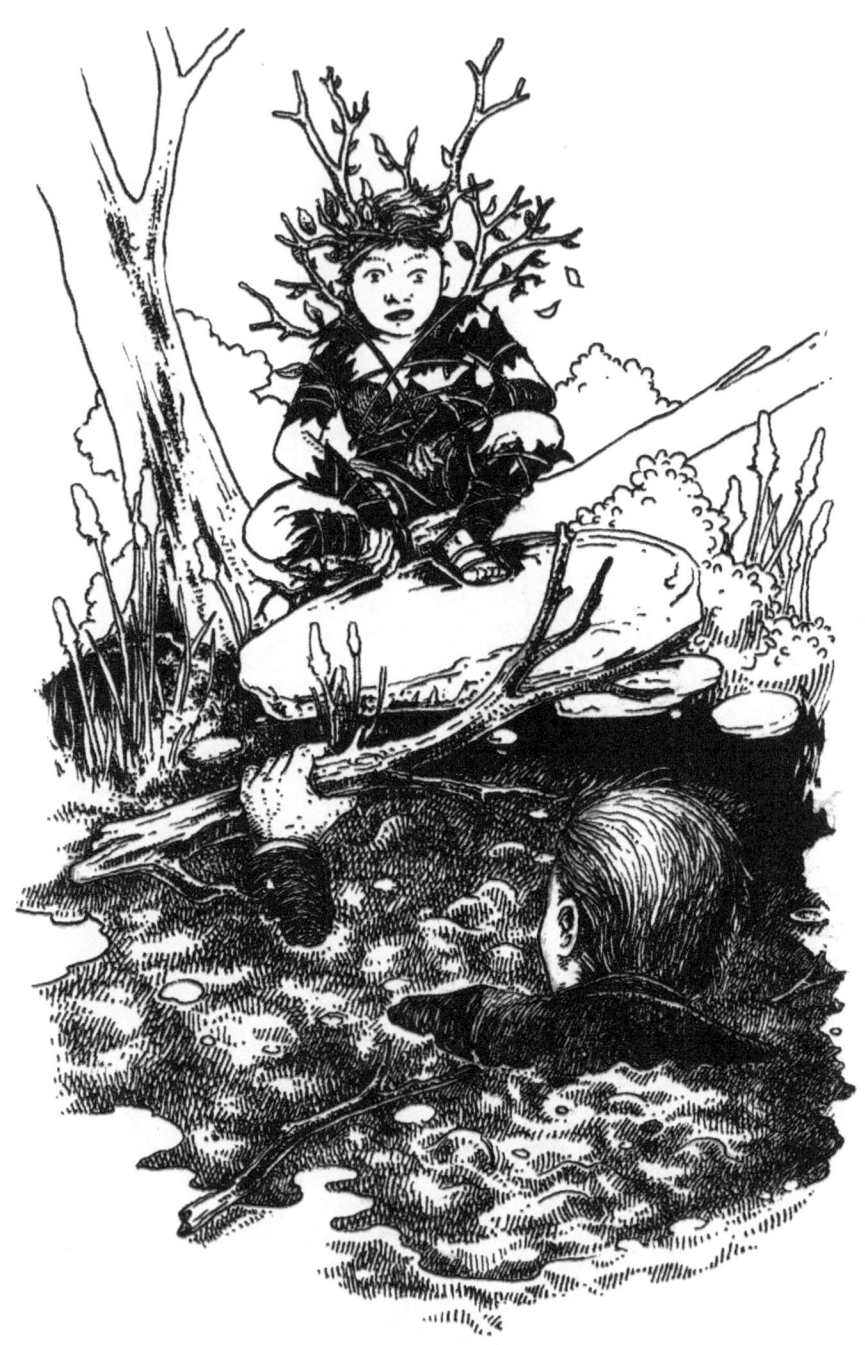

Stuck in mud

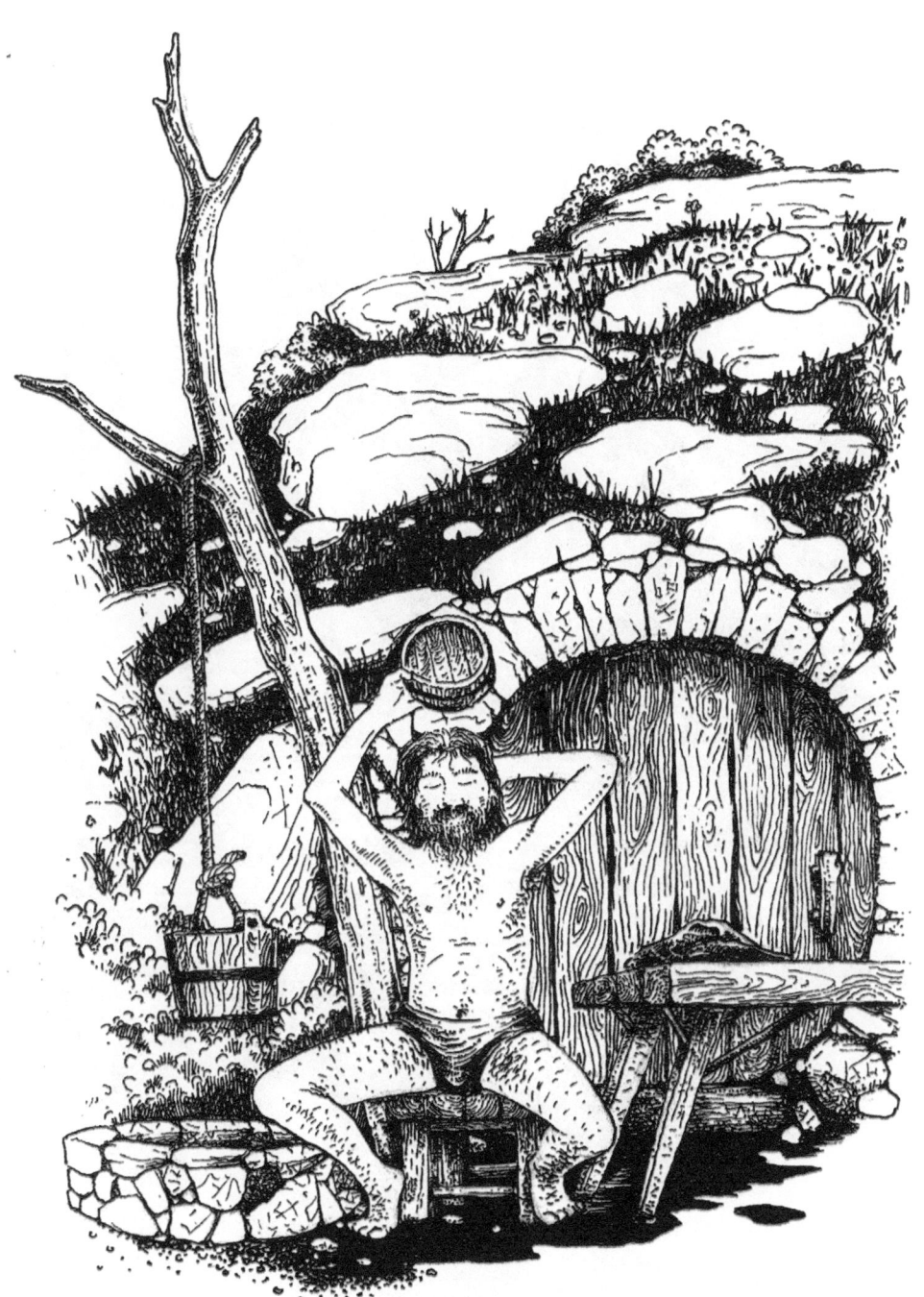

Old hermit

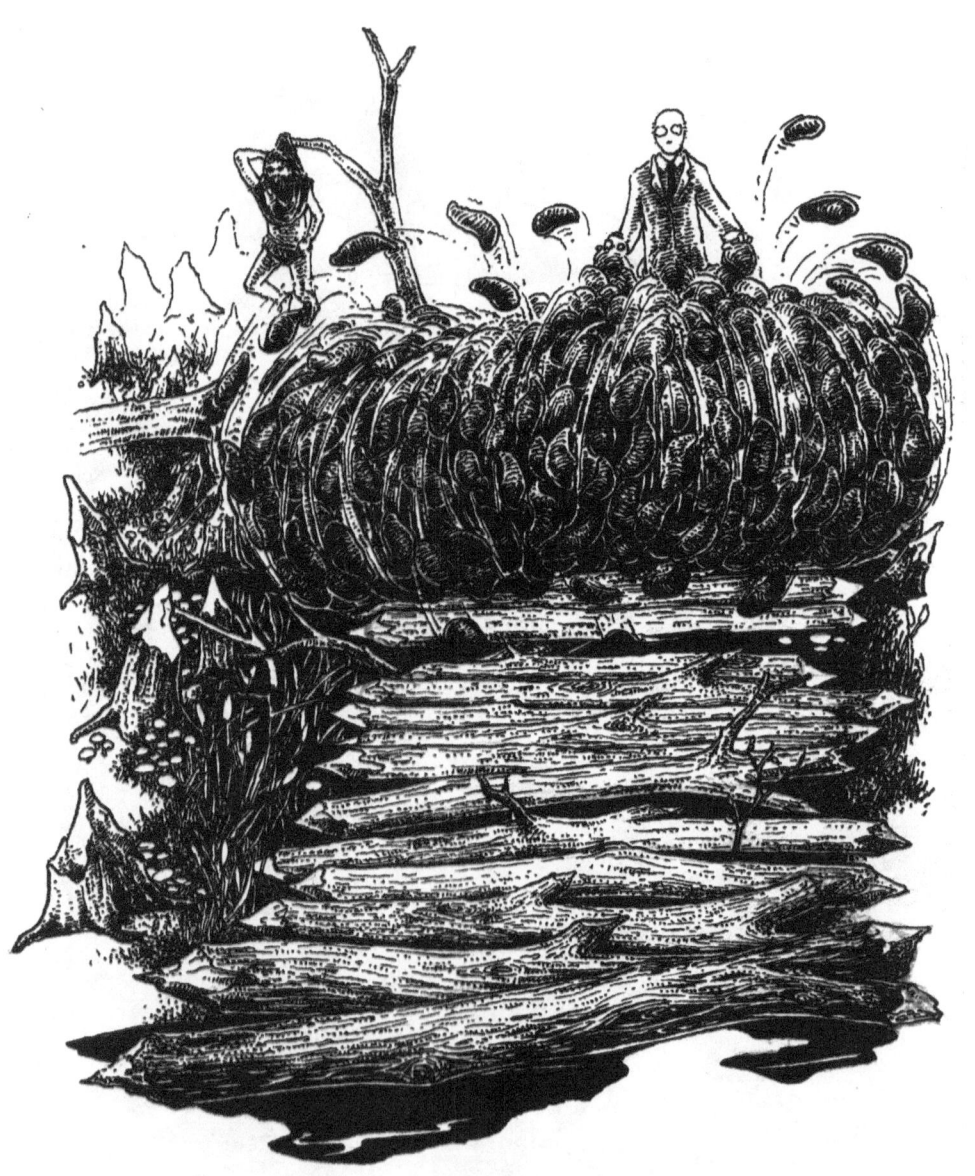

Bulldoze

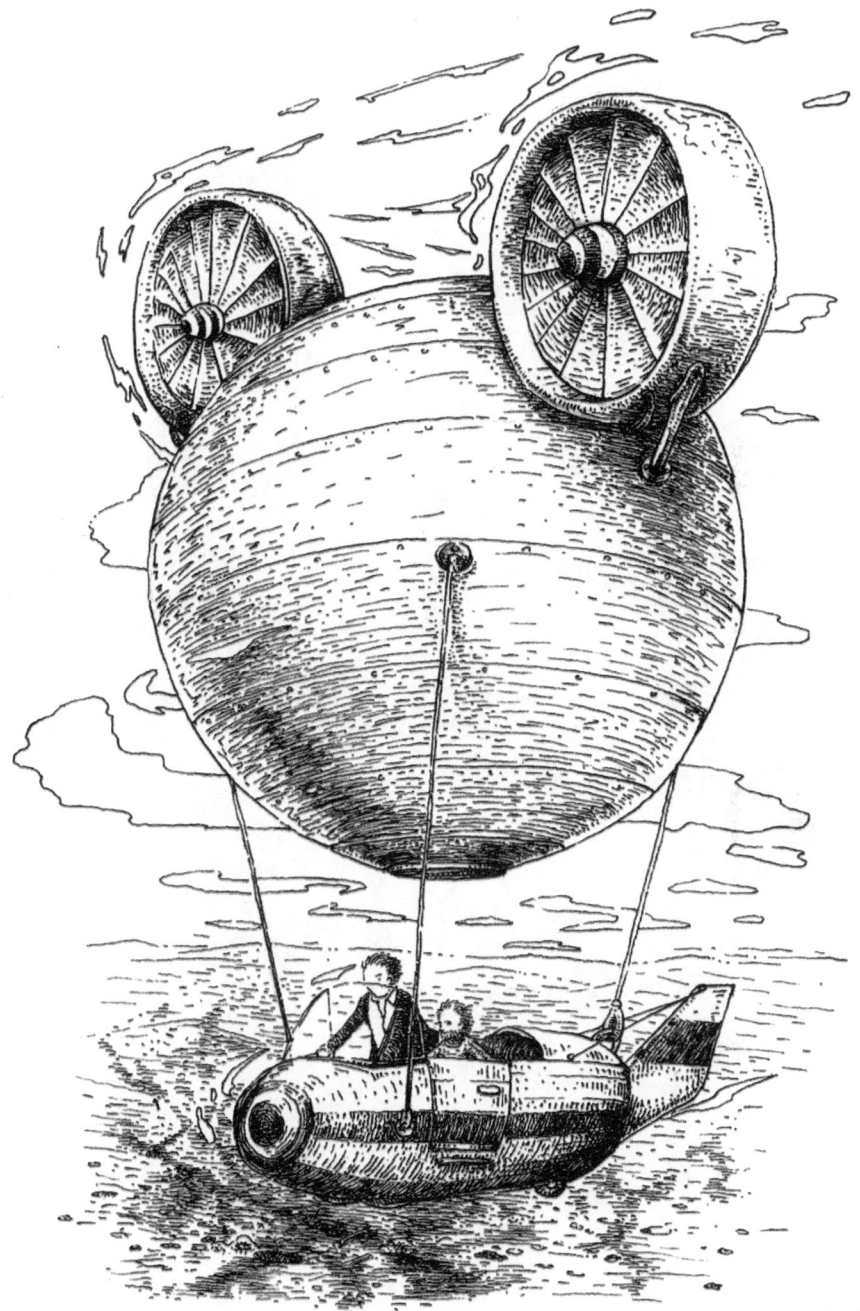

Advanced ballon

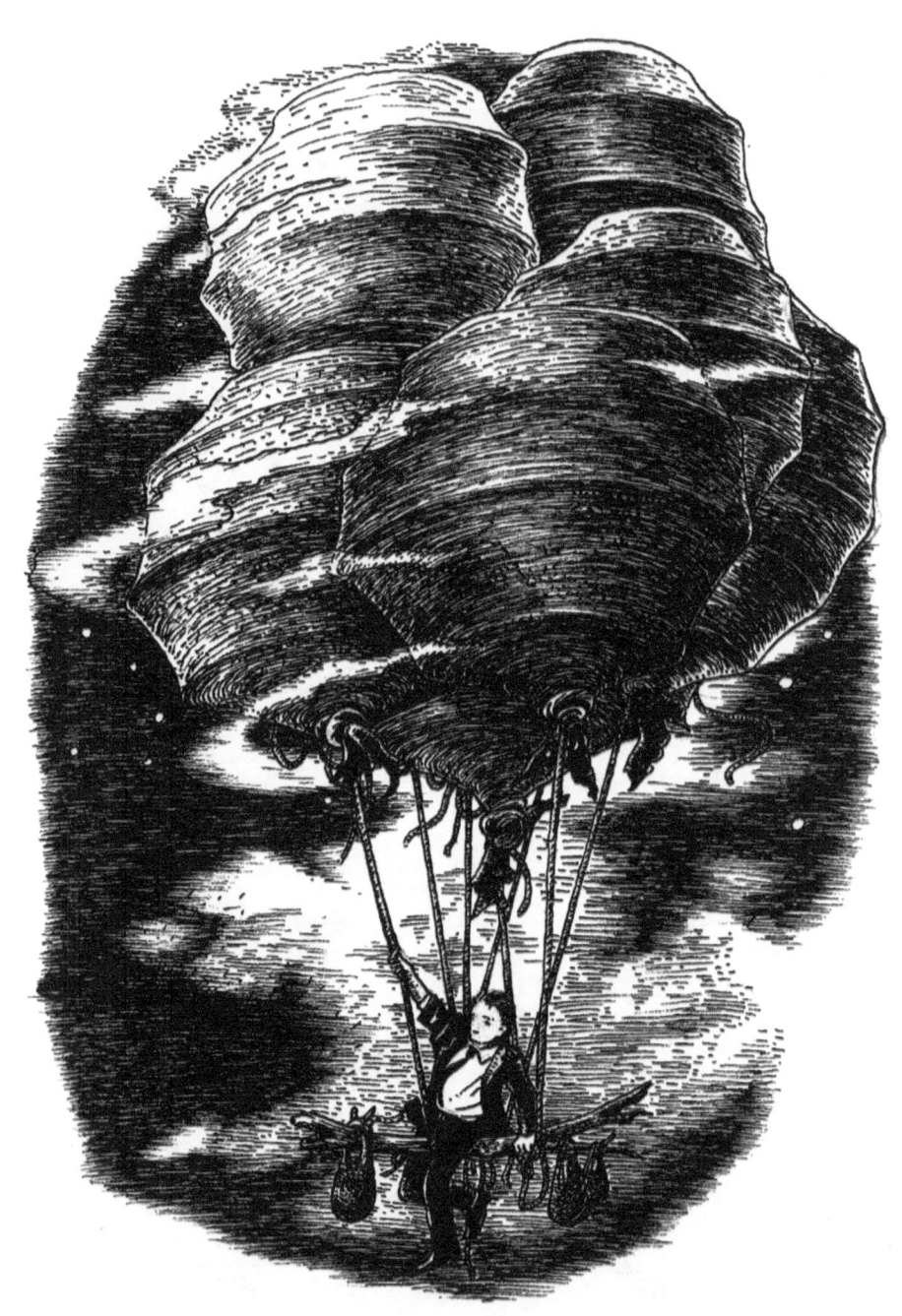

Primitive ballon

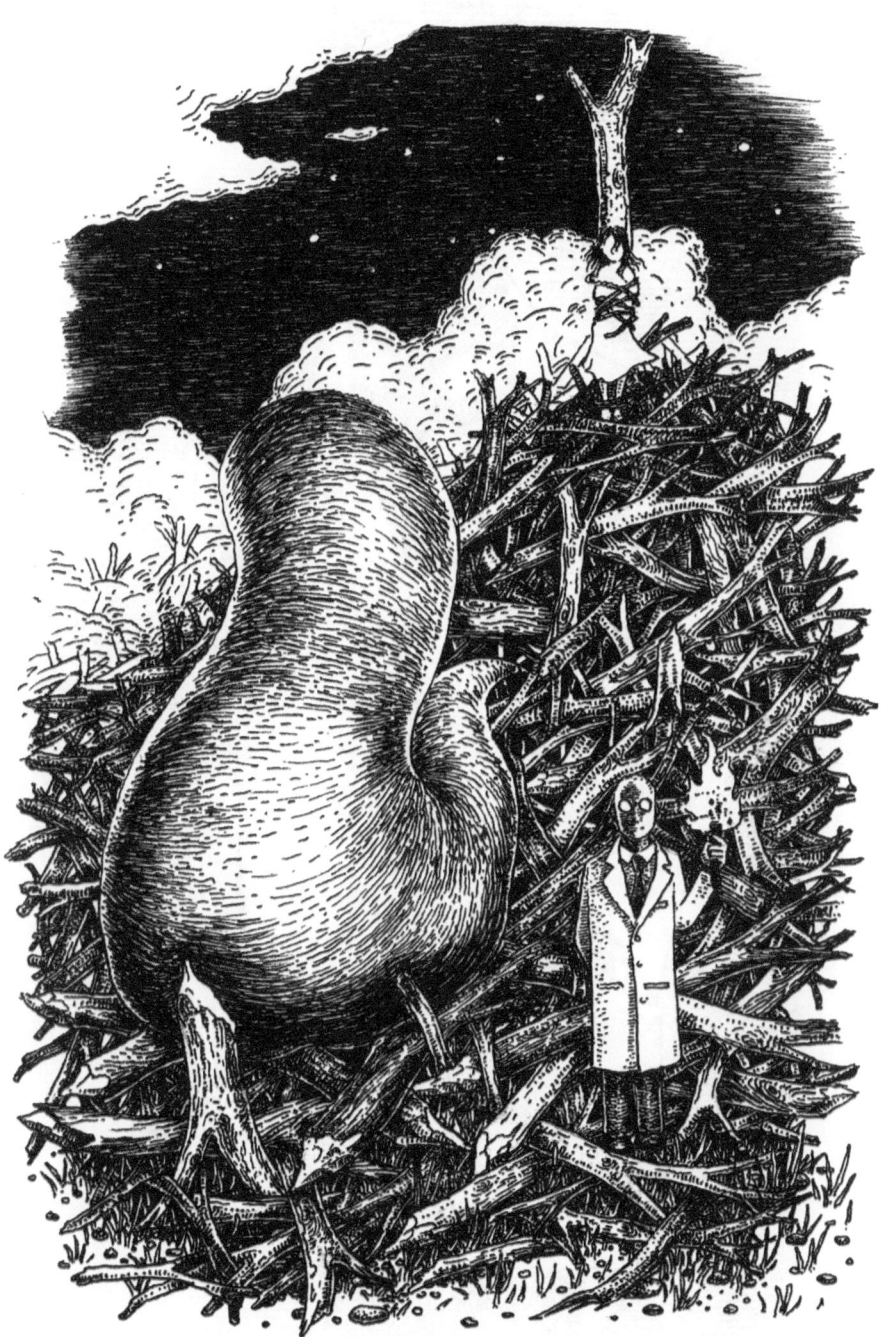

Wood pile

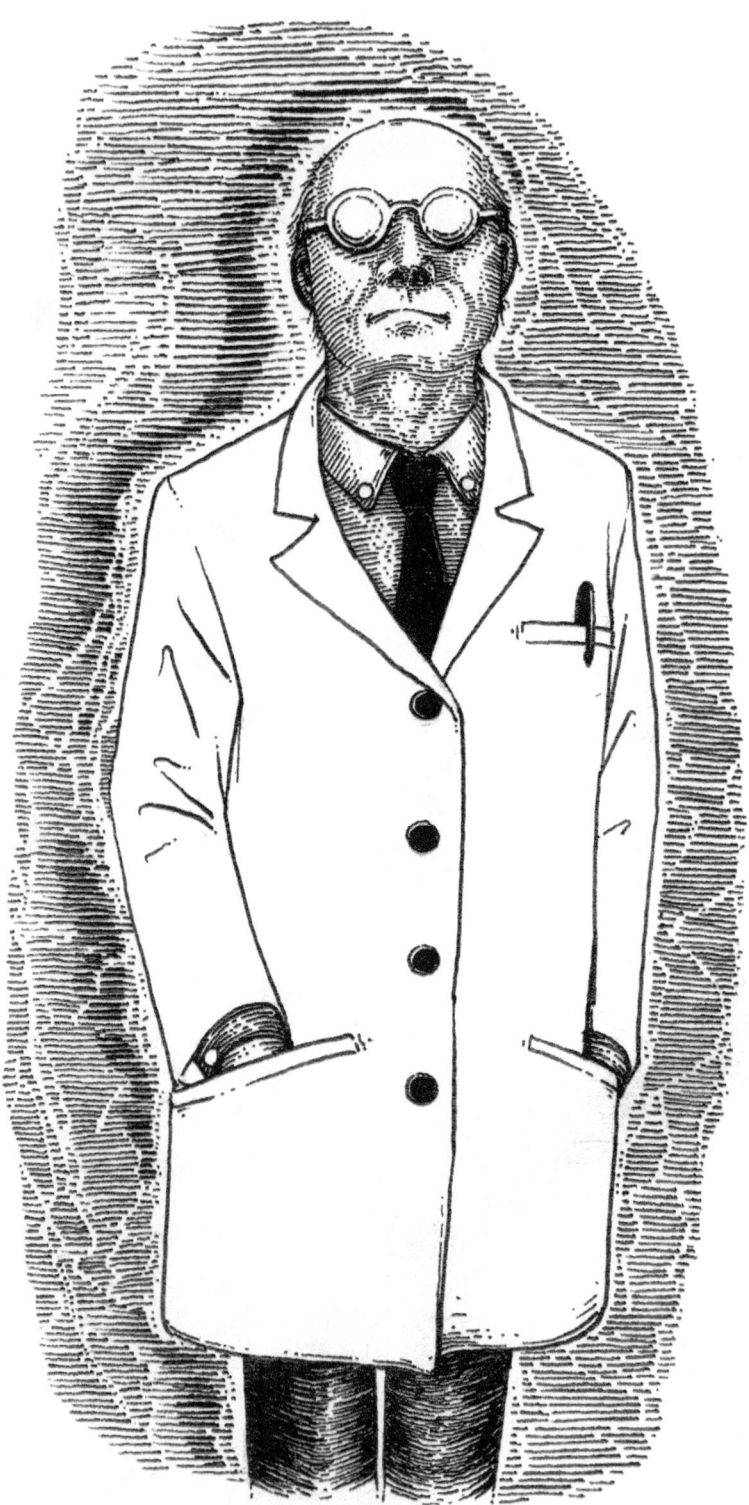

Doctor

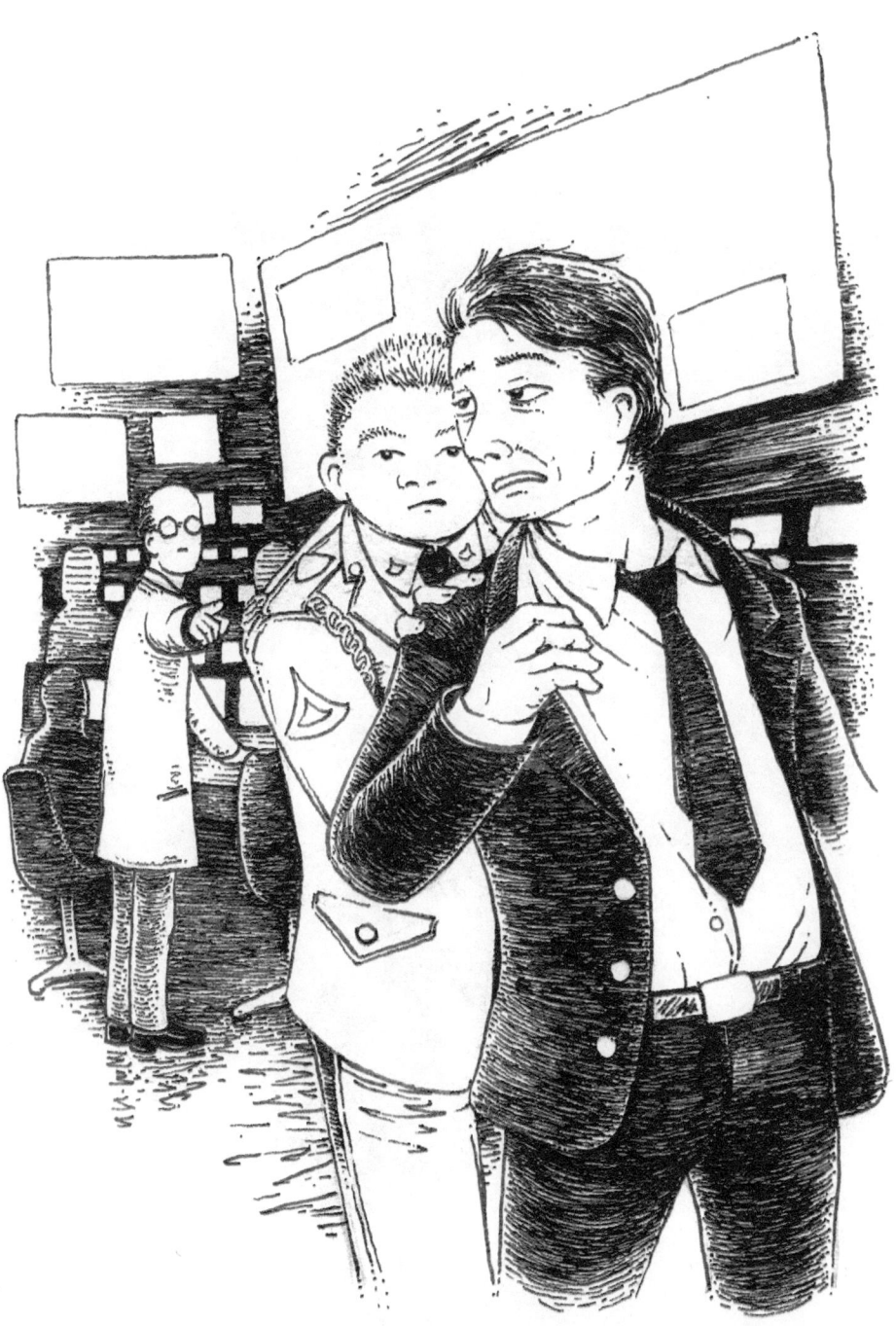

Control room

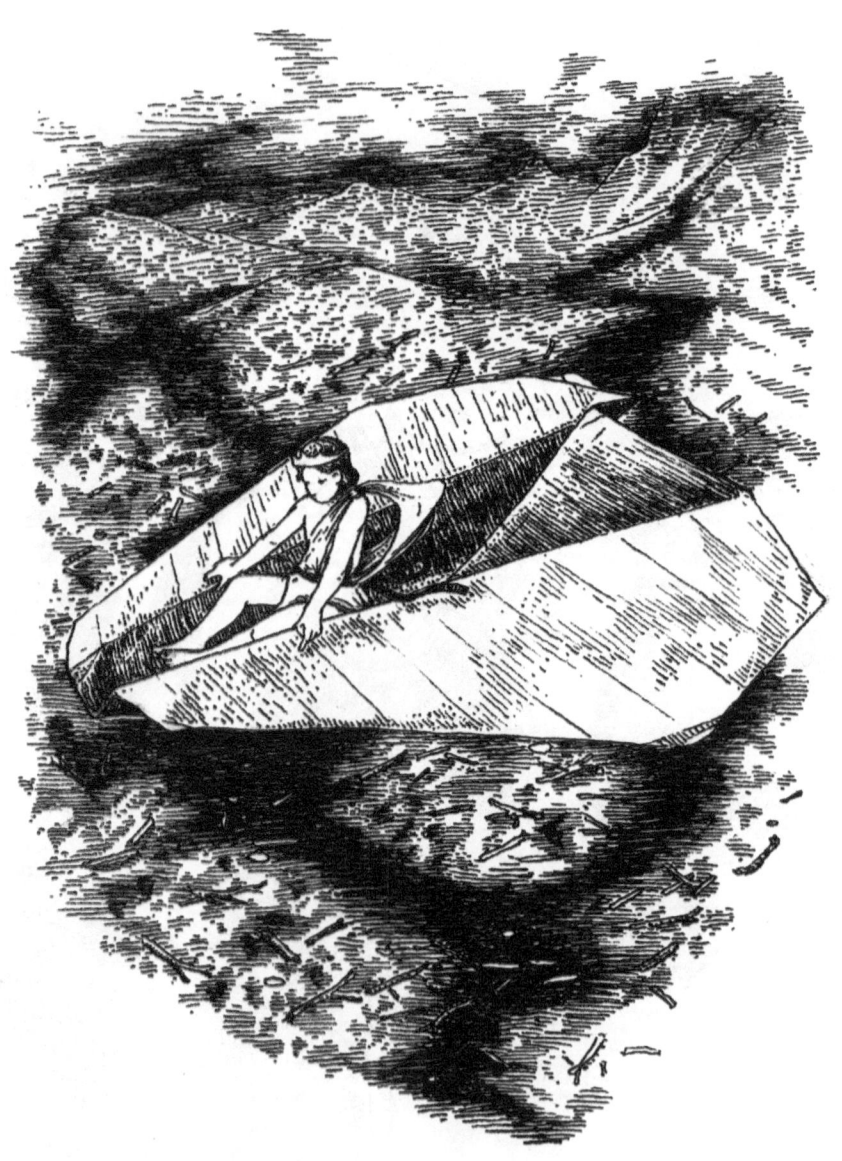

Paper plane

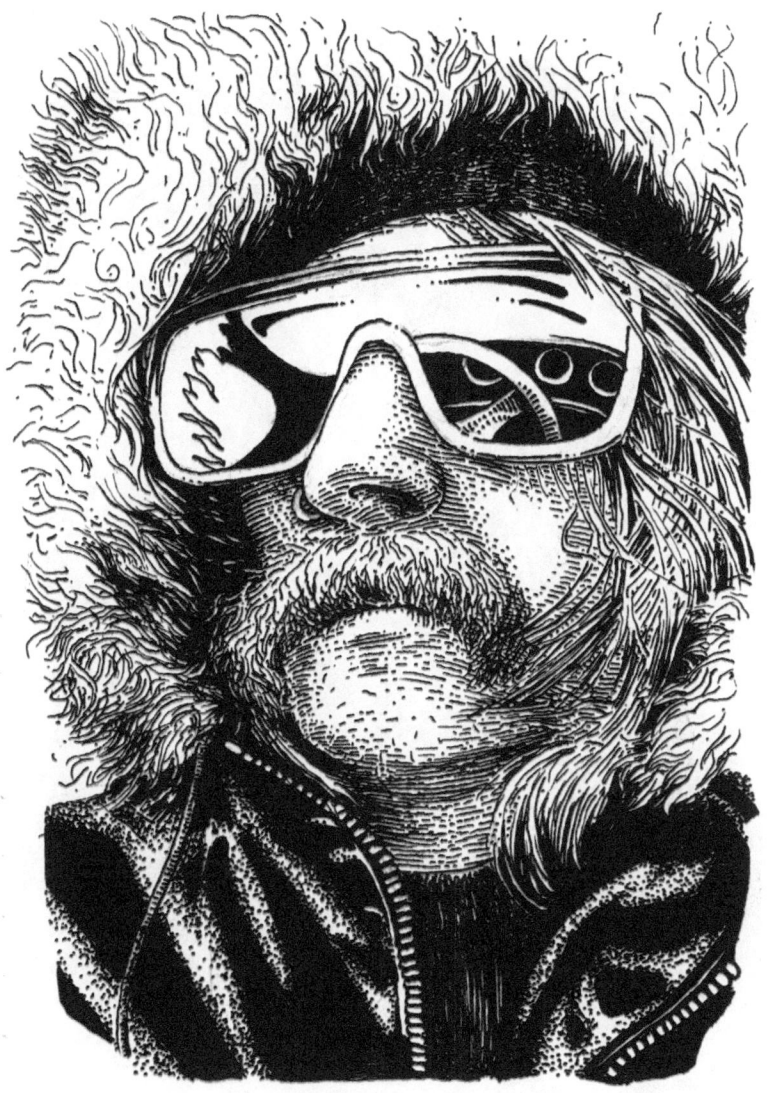

Drive

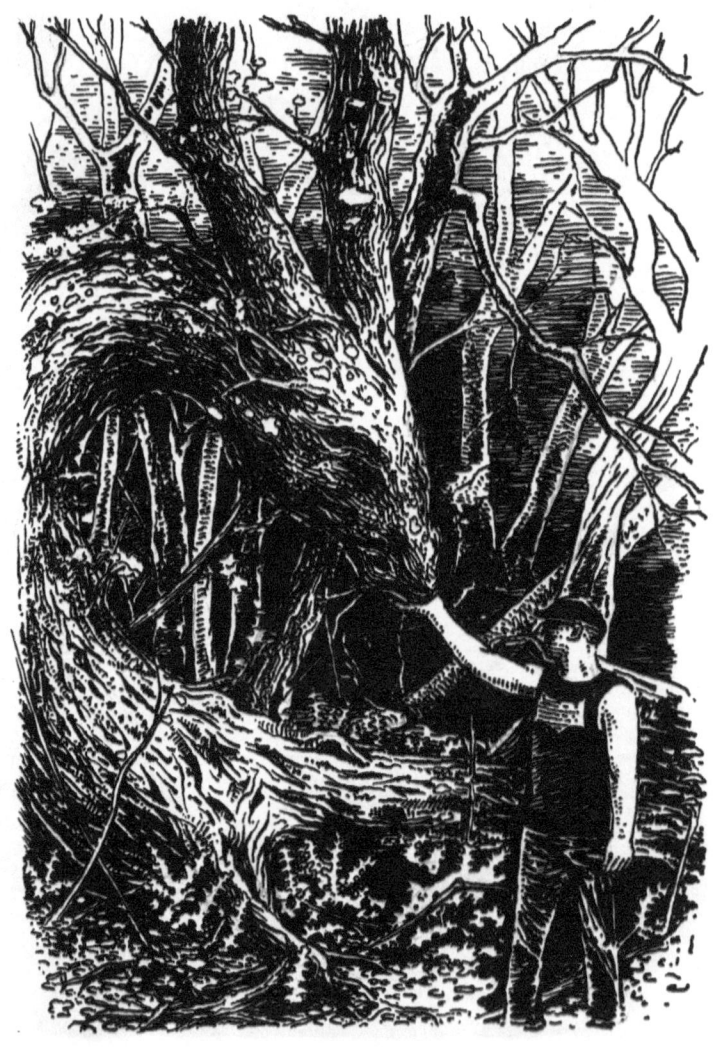

Forest dragon

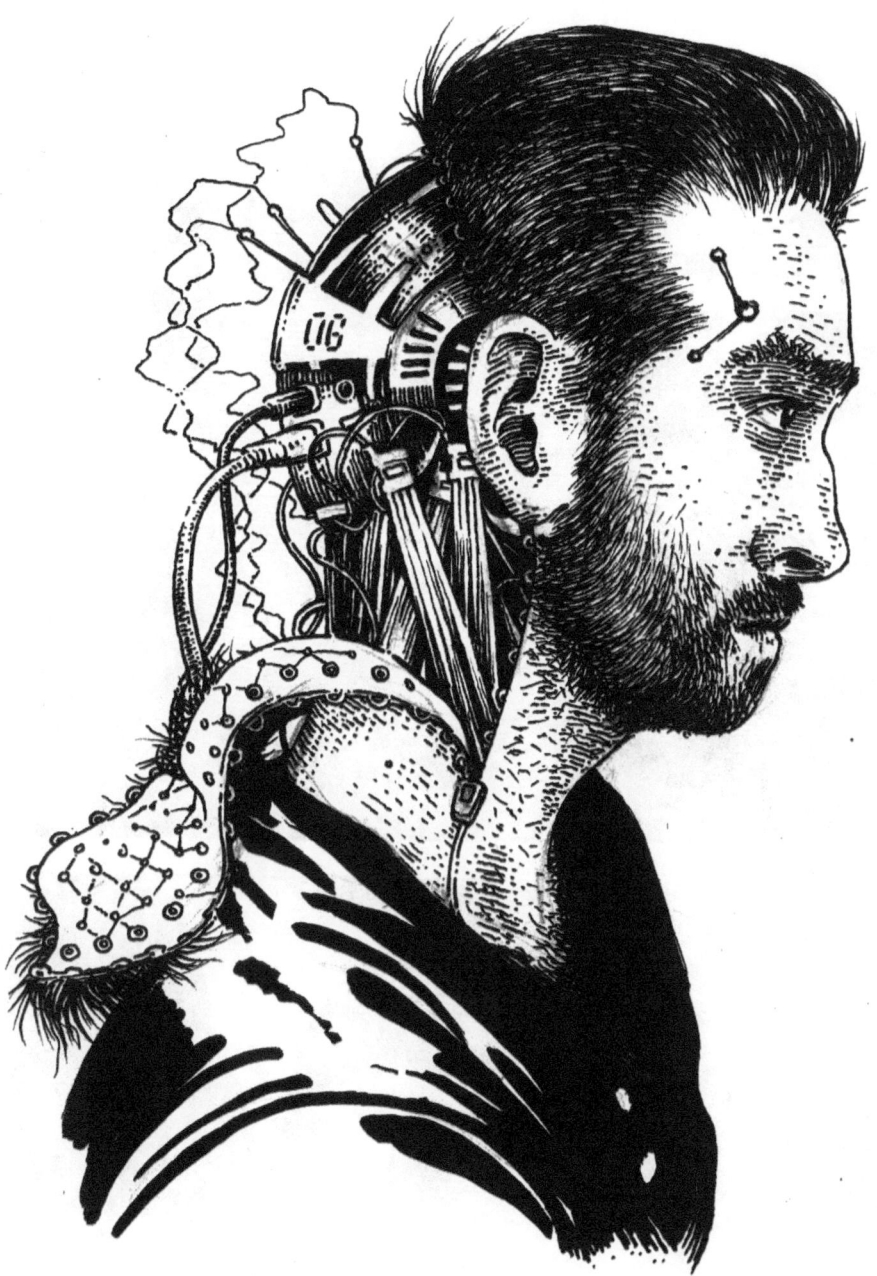

Connected

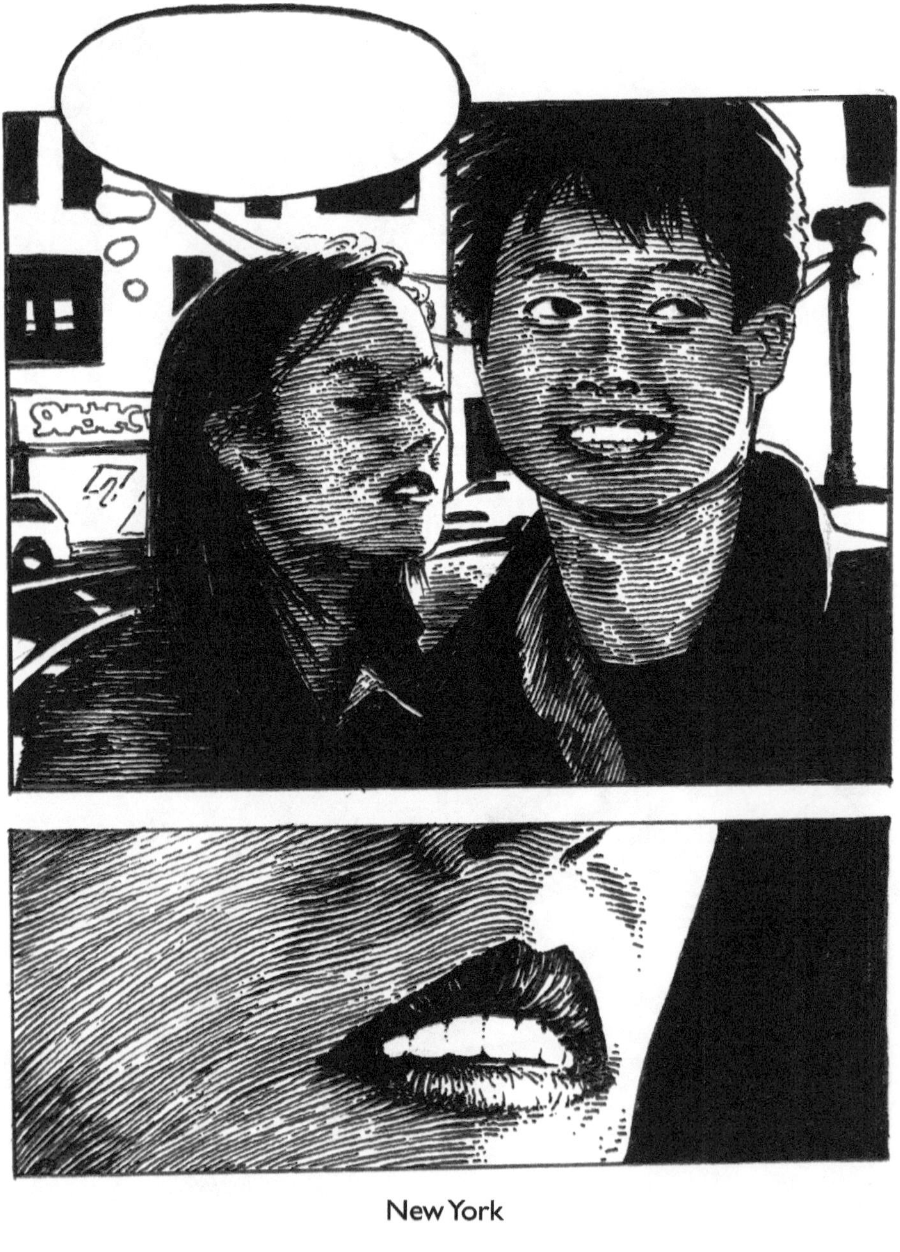

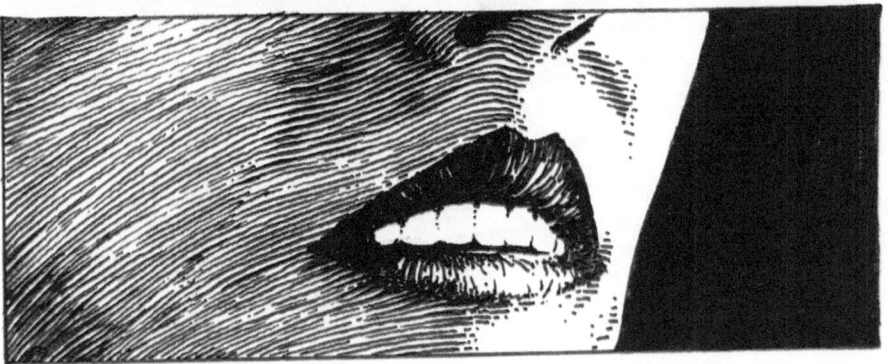

New York

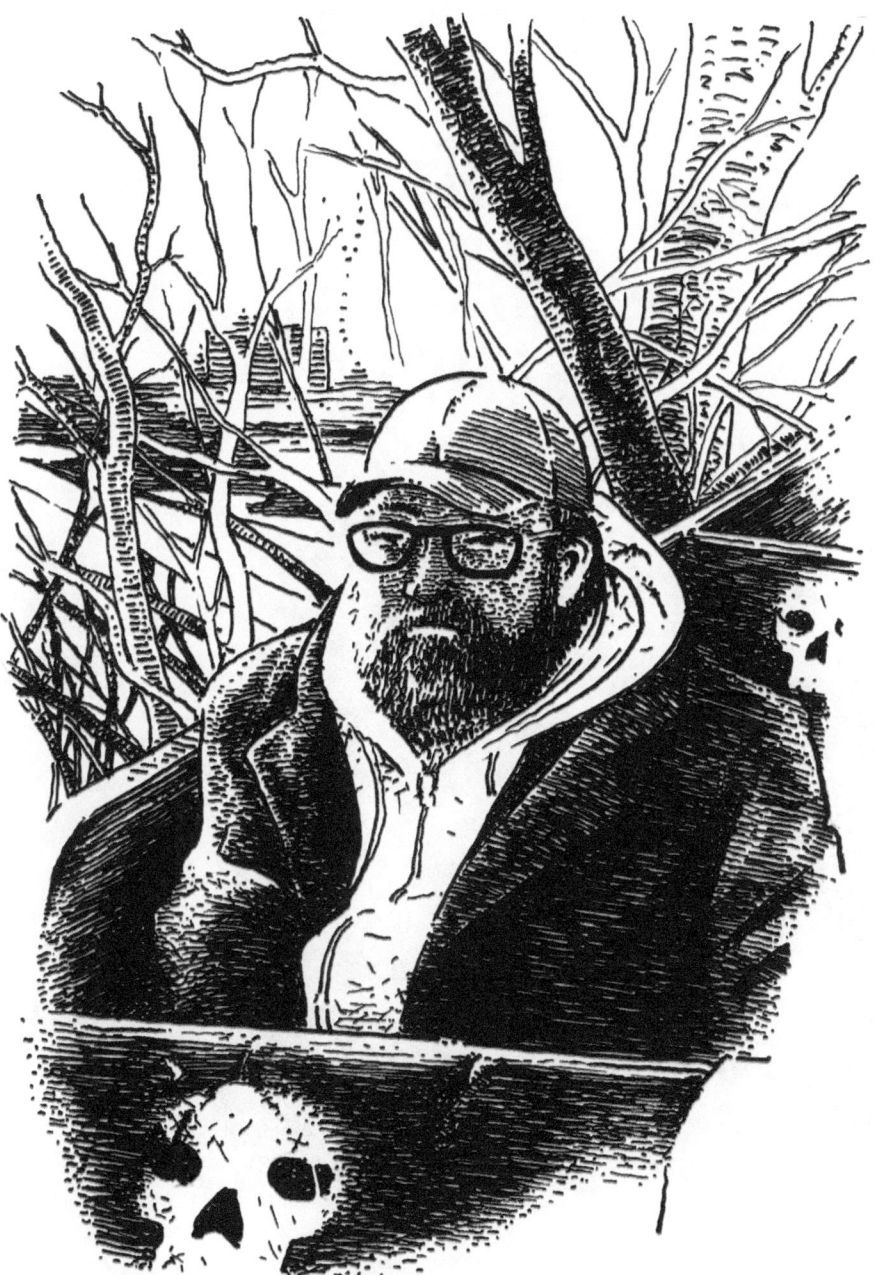

Depression

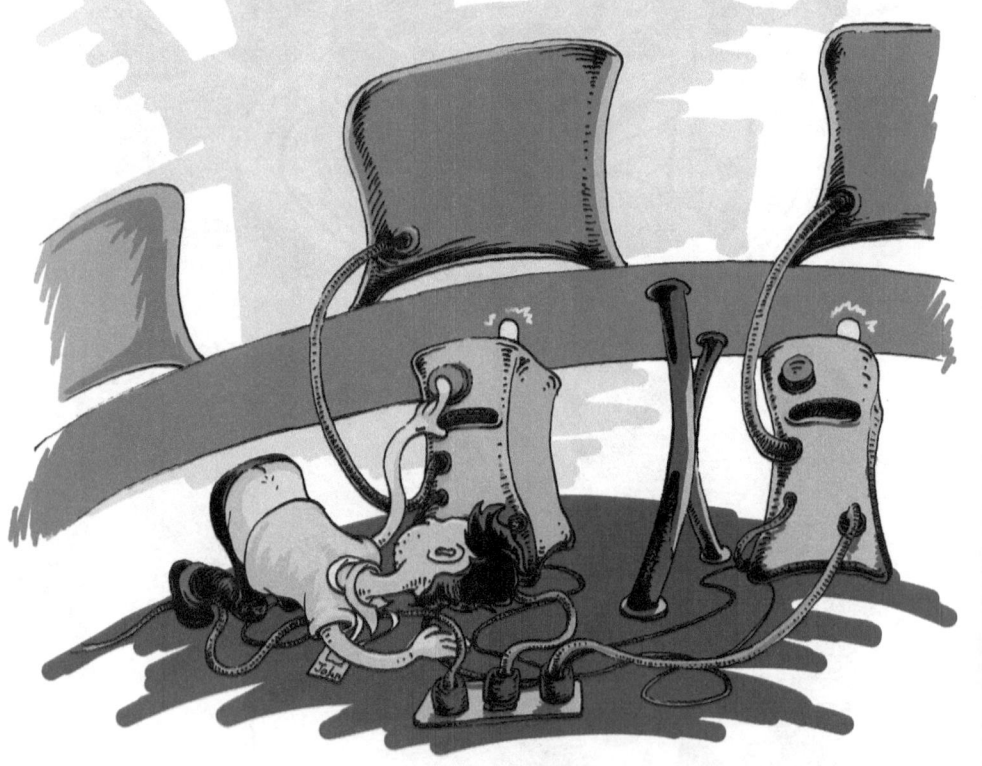

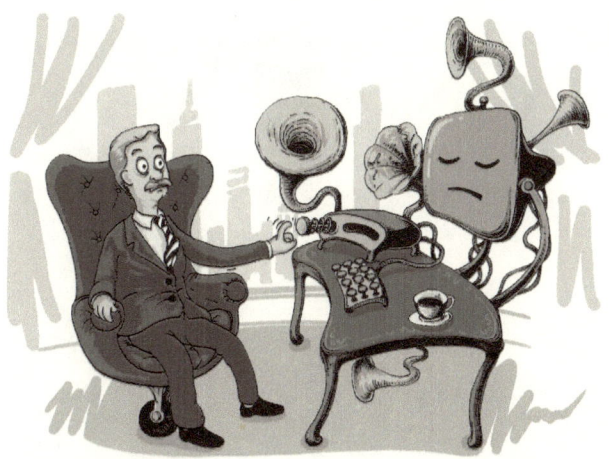

The Big Boss sat at his computing machine
And pressed the go-goer, a button of green.
But go did not go and the screen stayed dark black,
While Boss nearly suffered a third heart attack.

.

"Now how can I fix this?" lamented Big Boss.
"If I can't do payroll, the staff will be cross!
I'll call my IT guy to come on his scooter,
That computer wizard, that Johnny Astuter!"

.

A few moments later, young Johnny Astor
He scooted right in on his small, silver scooter.
"Well, what can I do here?" he said to the boss,
"Shall I wipe your nostrils, or help you to floss?"

.

"My compy-machine,"
said the boss with a hiss,
"It won't bleep and won't bloop.
There is something amiss!"
"Oh that's easy!" said Johnny,
and scratched at his chin.
"You've forgotten to plug this here
bleep-blooper in!"

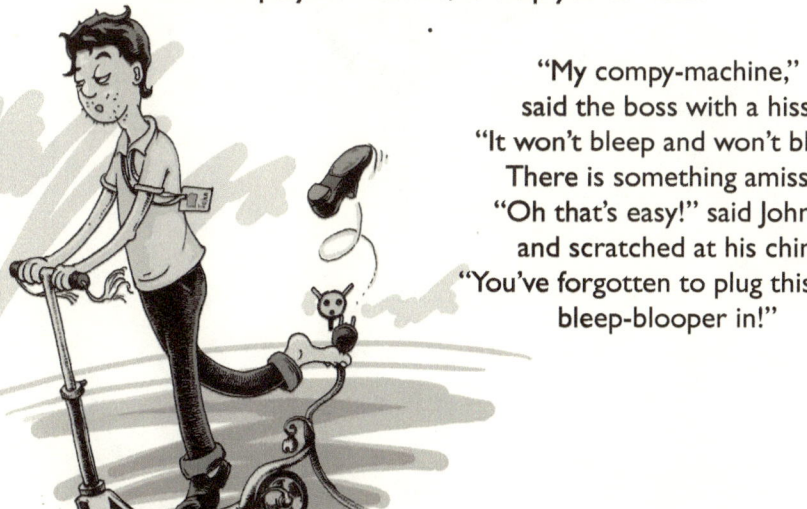

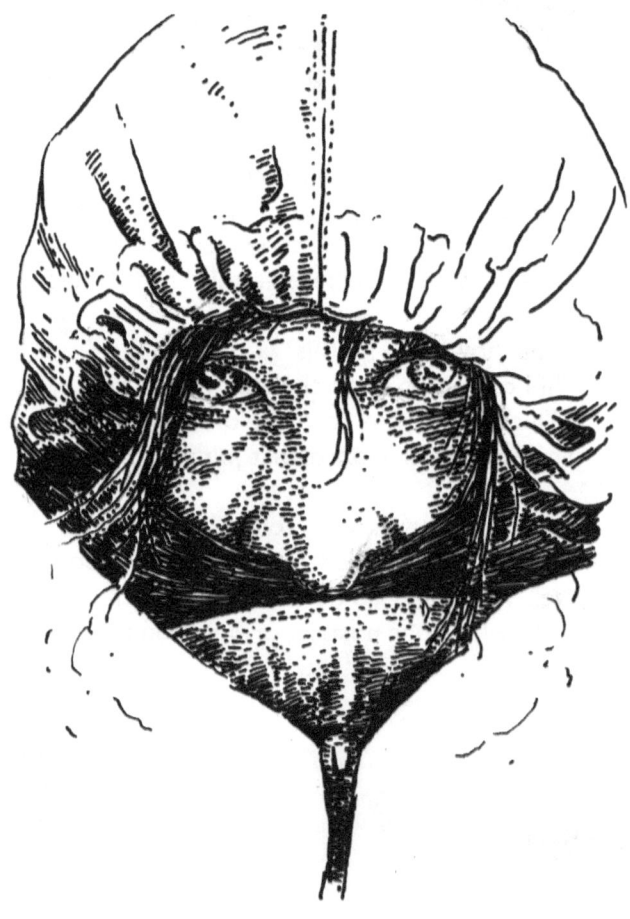

Cold

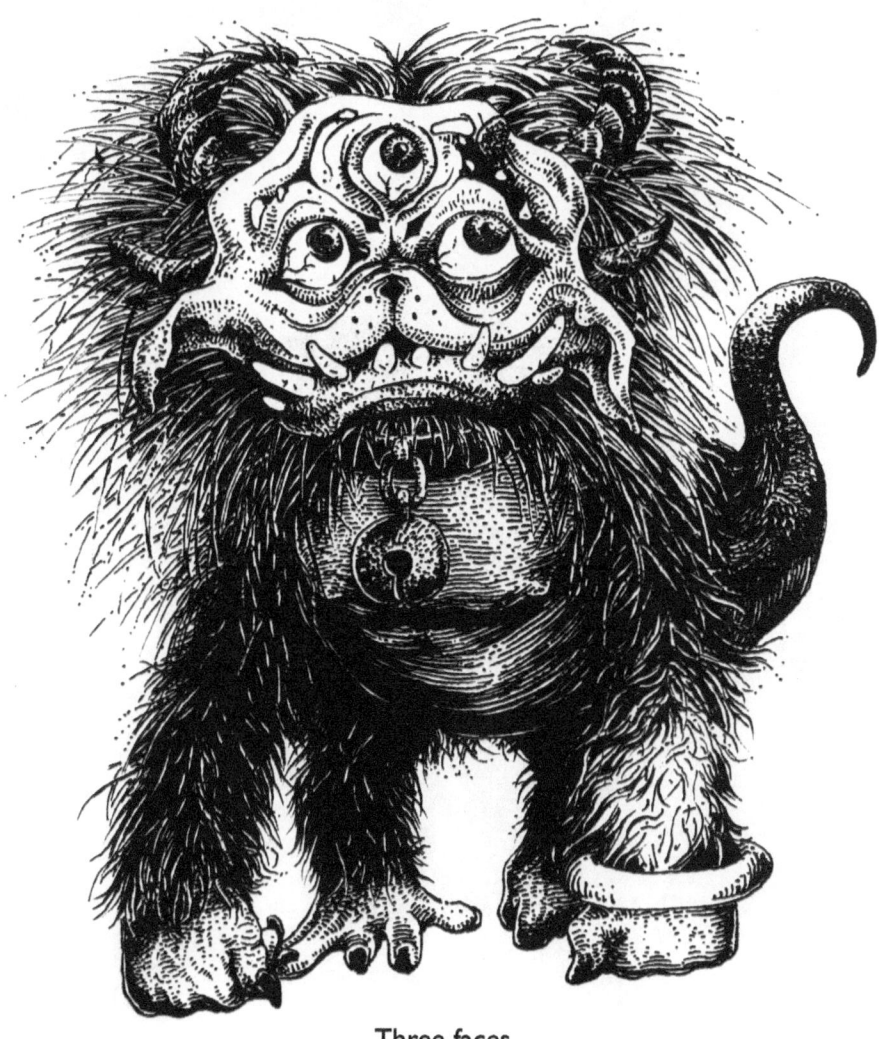

Three faces

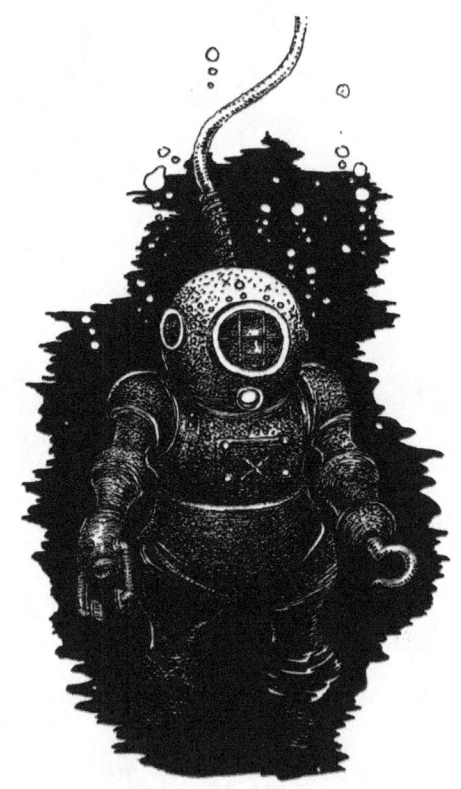

Diver

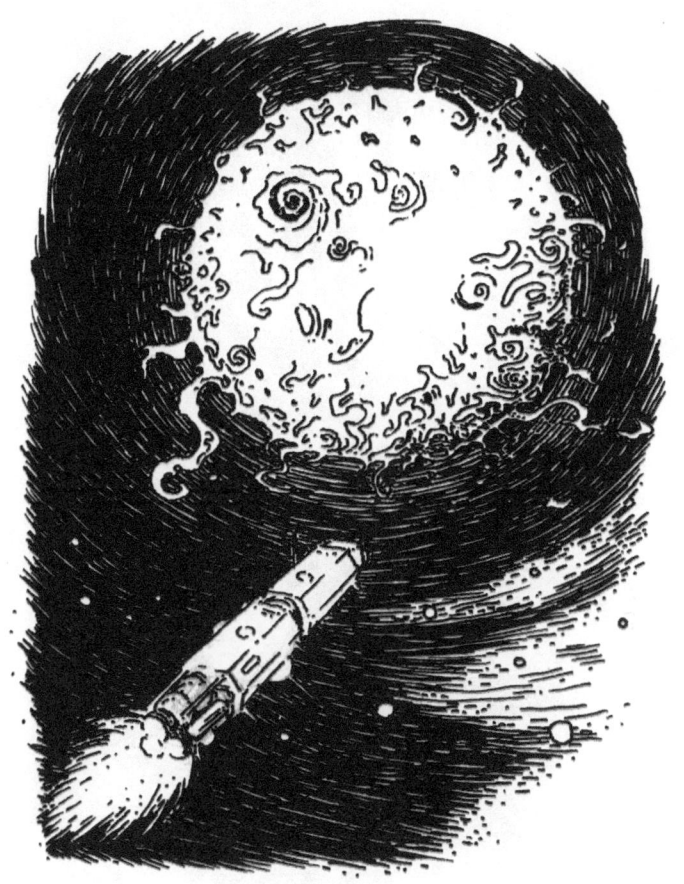

Rocket

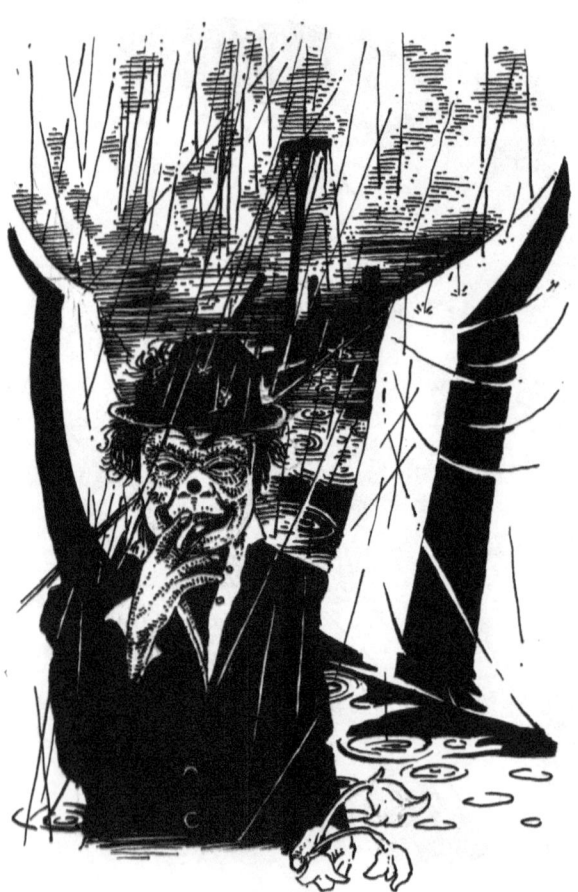

Clown

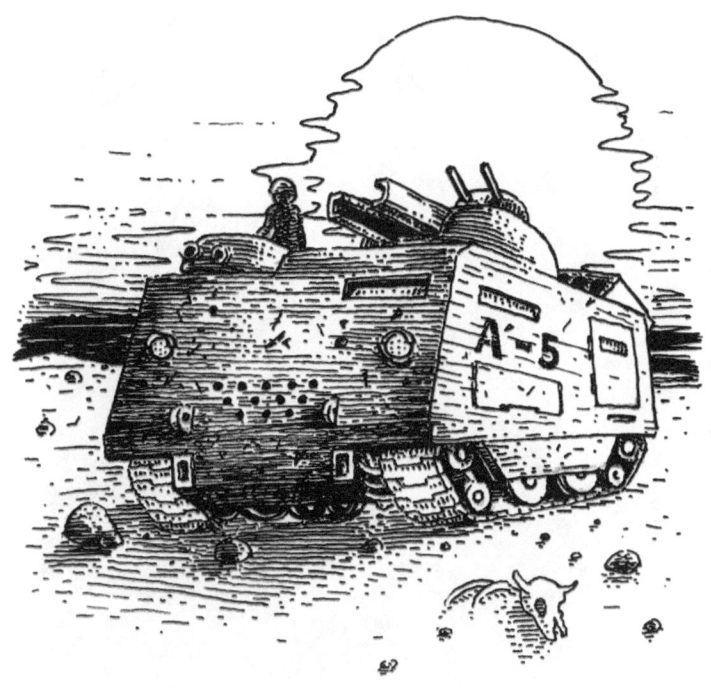

Armor

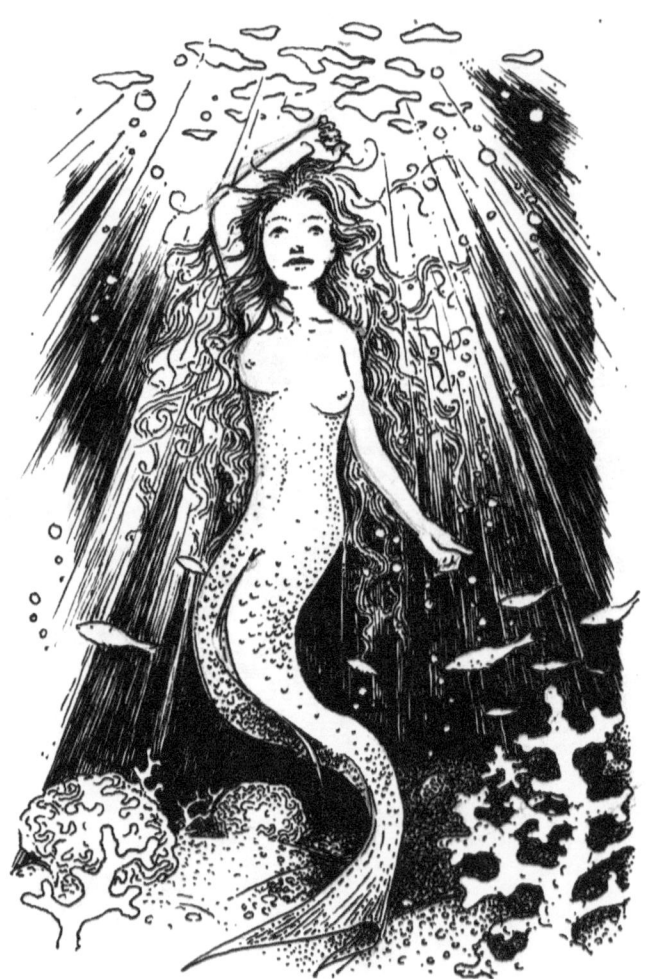

Mermaid

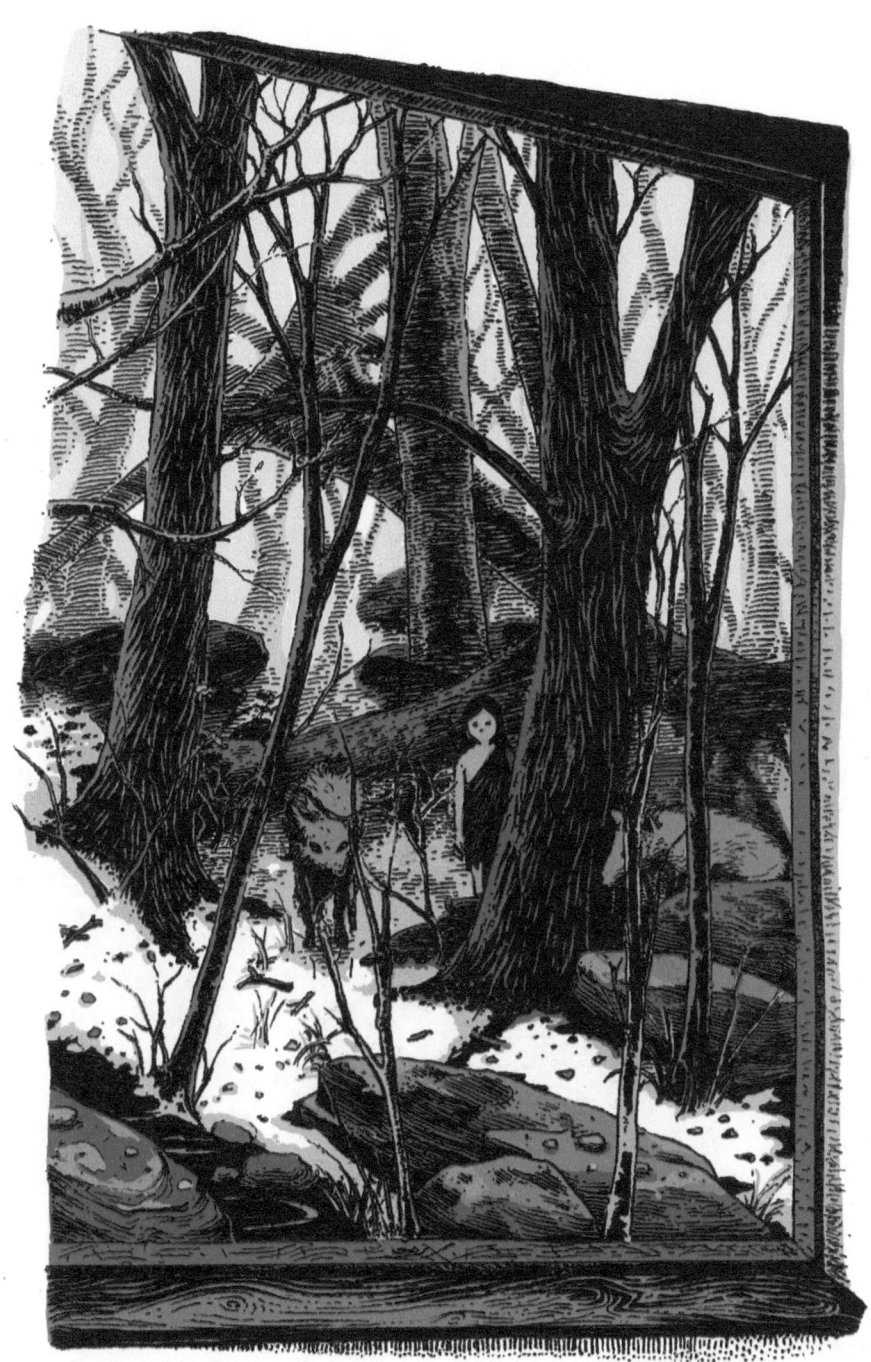

Bear mountain

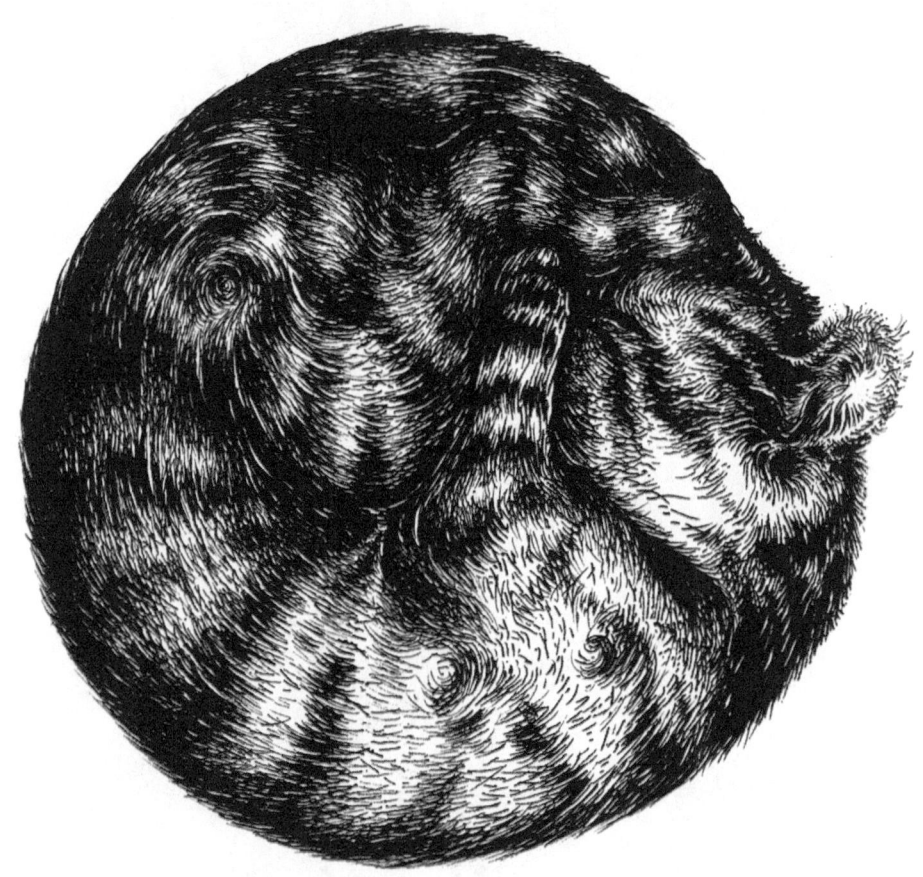

Cat

BEAST OF HOBOKEN

Y.F. 2011

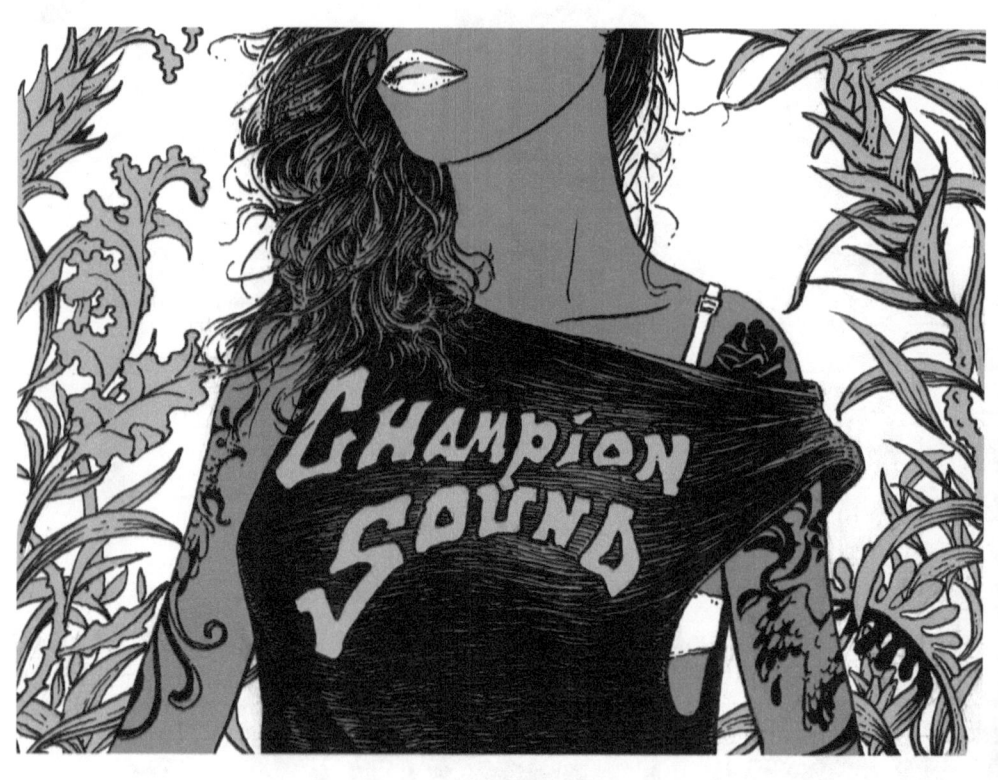

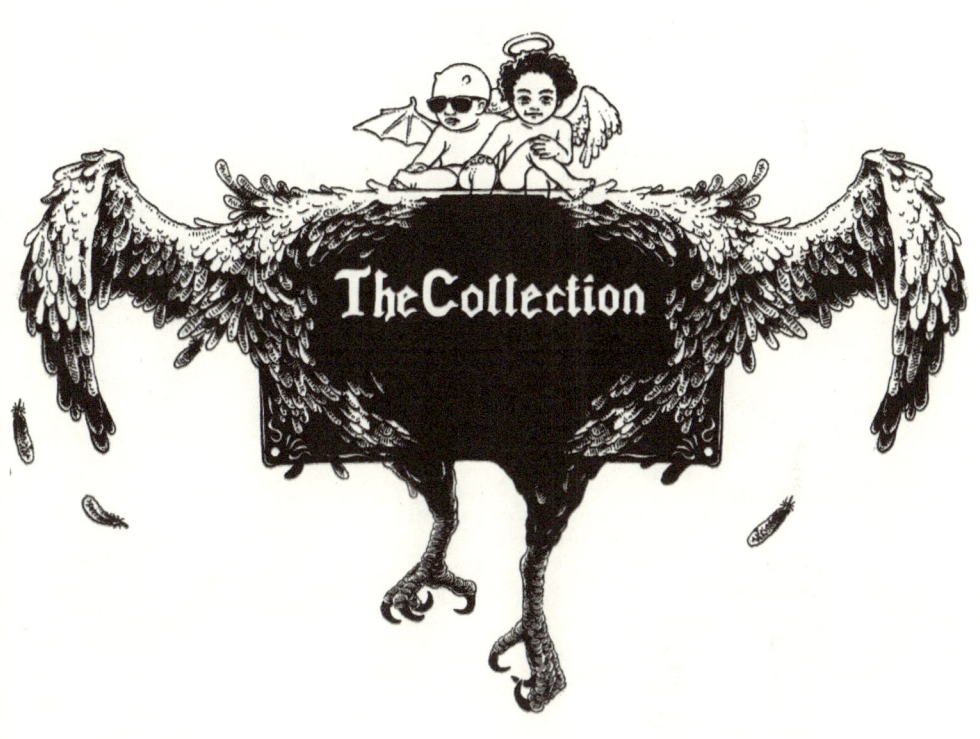

The End

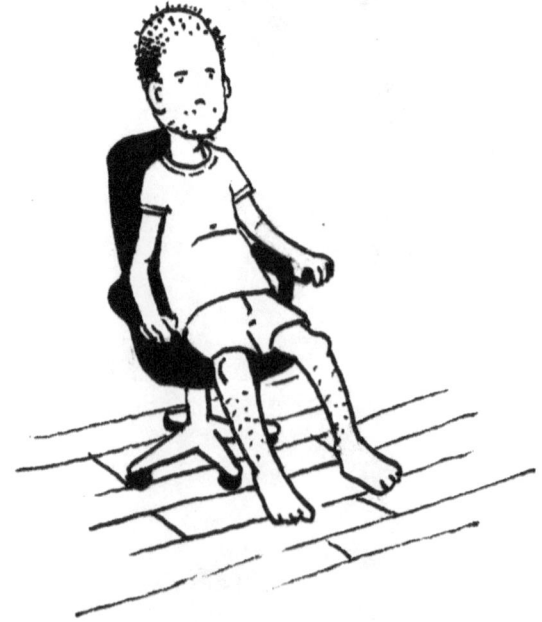